Bequeathed by Edith Wils

Published 1915

Please treat with care

Present-Day Gardening

EDITED BY . . . .
R. HOOPER PEARSON
MANAGING EDITOR
OF THE *GARDENERS'
CHRONICLE* . . . . .

A LIST OF VOLUMES
IN THE SERIES IS
GIVEN ON THE NEXT
PAGE. . . . .

Present-Day Gardening

List of Volumes in the Series.

1. SWEET PEAS. By HORACE J. WRIGHT, late Secretary and Chairman of the National Sweet Pea Society. With Chapter on "Sweet Peas for Exhibition" by THOS. STEVENSON. [Revised 1915.]
2. PANSIES, VIOLAS AND VIOLETS. By WILLIAM CUTHBERTSON, J.P., and R. HOOPER PEARSON.
3. ROOT AND STEM VEGETABLES. By ALEXANDER DEAN, V.M.H., Chairman of the National Vegetable Society.
4. DAFFODILS. By Rev. J. JACOB, Secretary of the Midland Daffodil Society, with Preface by the Rev. W. WILKS, M.A., Secretary of the Royal Horticultural Society.
5. ORCHIDS. By JAMES O'BRIEN, V.M.H., Secretary of the Orchid Committee of the Royal Horticultural Society.
6. CARNATIONS AND PINKS. By T. H. COOK Head Gardener to Queen Alexandra at Sandringham JAMES DOUGLAS, V.M.H.; and J. F. M'LEOD, Head Gardener to Mr. J Pierpont Morgan.
7. RHODODENDRONS AND AZALEAS. (*The first popular volume published on this subject.*) By WILLIAM WATSON, A.L.S., Curator of the Royal Botanic Gardens, Kew, with Preface by Sir FRED. W. MOORE, M.A., A.L.S., V.M.H.
8. LILIES. By A. GROVE, F.L.S., with Preface by H. J. ELWES, F.R.S.
9. APPLES AND PEARS. By GEORGE BUNYARD, V.M.H., Chairman of Fruit and Vegetable Committee of Royal Horticultural Society.
10. ROSES. By H. R. DARLINGTON, Vice-President of National Rose Society. (*Double volume.*)
11. IRISES. By W. RICKATSON DYKES, M.A., L.-ès-L. With Preface by PROFESSOR I. BAYLEY BALFOUR, D.Sc., F.R.S., &c.
12. ANNUALS, HARDY AND HALF-HARDY. By C. H. CURTIS, Hon. Sec. of the National Sweet Pea Society.
13. CHRYSANTHEMUMS. By THOMAS STEVENSON, with chapters by C. HARMAN PAYNE and CHARLES E. SHEA.
14. TULIPS. (*The first volume on the subject in the English language.*) By Rev. J. JACOB, Member of R.H.S. Narcissus and Tulip Committee.
15. THE ROCK GARDEN. By REGINALD FARRER, Author of "Among the Hills," "My Rock Garden," "In a Yorkshire Garden," &c., with Preface by J. BRETLAND FARMER, D.Sc., F.R.S
16. DAHLIAS. By GEORGE GORDON, V.M.H., President of the National Dahlia Society.
17. CLIMBING PLANTS. By WILLIAM WATSON, Curator of Royal Botanic Gardens, Kew. With Introduction by W. ROBINSON.

These will be followed by volumes on **Trees and Shrubs, Window Gardens, Pæonies, Primulas, Cucumbers, Melons, Bedding Plants, Hardy Herbaceous Plants, Ferns, Tomatoes, Bulbous Plants, Peaches and Nectarines, Vines, Stove and Greenhouse Plants, &c.**

PLATE I (*Frontispiece*)

PASSIFLORA CŒRULEA "CONSTANCE ELLIOTT"

Climbing Plants

By

William Watson

With Introduction by

W. Robinson

Author of "The English Flower Garden"

London: T. C. & E. C. Jack
67 Long Acre, W.C., & Edinburgh

CONTENTS

LIST OF ILLUSTRATIONS

COLOURED PLATES

BLACK AND WHITE PLATES

CLIMBING PLANTS

INTRODUCTION

A HANDY treatise on climbing plants for gardens is a welcome addition to garden books. Mr. Watson has for many years lived among climbers from all parts of the world. His chapters on the best climbers for gardens and greenhouses will be useful to all lovers of horticulture. A clear fact in our gardening is that but little of the infinite variety and beauty of the climber is seen in many gardens; this book should help to a change for the better.

After the gift of trees of the earth-mother, the greatest for the gardener are the climbers that adorn them with infinite grace. It is needless to describe their beauty. Botanical and gardening descriptions of them are numerous, and nurserymen send out attractive lists of them. So all is well except their cultivation, which is often a dismal failure. Impressed with the fact that in many large gardens it was rare to see a trace of the beauty of climbing plants, and wondering why it was so, I began to make little experiments; first of all, and in obedience to their natural habit, which is to grow on trees and bushes in many lands of mountain copse and shore, I have planted them in every position, from an orchard hedgerow to a grove of Magnolias, and have had much success.

The plan was to plant one at the base of some shrub or tree in obedience to the natural habit of the climber, and this is best done when the trees and shrubs are young and the ground is fresh, but I have done it in all conditions. Sometimes a tree or shrub overpowers the plant, but this will not happen to the freer kinds, like the Indian species of Clematis, which are so vigorous that one needs have no fear of them. They are easily raised from seed also, so that one is spared the trouble which comes from grafting. Most interest, however, came from getting the larger-flowered Japanese or Chinese species into picturesque and artistic ways. These plants creep up the tree unaided by training or staking, and if not as vigorous as they would be if planted by themselves, they are even more beautiful to see in the light and shadow of the tree.

The European Clematis is very free, and will grow in a hedgerow. In making a fence of live plants round an orchard, which is the only right way to fence, we sowed a few seeds of these, and every year they have been a charm, showing sprays of flowers above the hedge as free as the foam of a wave. The yellow sorts, like *C. tangutica*, are well fitted for this kind of planting, and not so well for the flower garden, being too vigorous. I tried all the kinds of Clematis I could get, and nearly everyone proved a success. Sir Harry Veitch sent me a set of the new Chinese species, and they grew like briars. They are not particular as to soil so long as it is open. In the flower garden we have to keep to the more fragile kinds, which, when grown on their own roots, give us thousands of flowers. We have to cut away the decayed parts in the autumn, and that is the only form of pruning these get! Clematises on trees we never think of pruning. More words have been wasted about pruning than about anything else in gardening.

I lately read in one of the great morning papers elaborate directions for pruning Clematises ; whether one should prune last year's growth, or this year's growth, or some other year's growth. It was probably written by one of the "lady students" at some horticultural college. If we had one here we could hardly place her forty feet high in a Corsican pine to prune a Clematis. By giving up all pruning trouble is saved, and one gets a more picturesque result. We have plants on walls and in all sorts of positions, and we have had no serious losses, though sometimes a holly or an apple-tree may have been weakened a little.

For climbers on walls the great thing is to see that the trees are not crucified, and that the natural toss of the plant is allowed full play. The best way to secure such a result is to use oak or chestnut battens in a rough simple way, and tie the shoots to them. All that misery of nailing with shreds with cold fingers on frosty mornings should go. It is not enough to have healthy plants ; one must also show their grace of form. The strongest and best of all ties is the red willow shoot. A few dozen red willows in a wet hollow will furnish a useful stock of withies cheaper and better than the grocer's tarred twine.

It is a mistake to clothe walls with climbers that do not need any such comfort. Ivy, for instance, is often used in this way, although it will grow in the woods, on rocks, on rough banks, and in many other places. Ivy should not be put on a house or wall, nor should we use the rougher and coarser Clematises, or even the Indian *C. montana,* in that way. It is a common mistake to suppose that the north side of walls is against success with many things, for they may be better off on the north than the south side. One of the most beautiful climbers I have ever seen was a Lapageria on the north side of a wall at Caerheys. The finest tea roses, too, are happy on the north side of a wall.

After various trials with Bamboo and wire and iron I came to the conclusion that the best trellising can be made from battens of our native Oak. Iron wire is not good, and the galvanised wire is not any better, but stout pencil-like wire may serve as a base for the smaller pieces of wood.

The vines of Northern Japan and China are a perfect treasure-house of climbers that may be grown almost anywhere. I was so much taken with them that when planting an orchard I put vines on the apple and other trees with superb effect. A "practical" friend who came along said, "What about the apples?" I said I did not care. As it happened, I got both the beauty of the vines and the apples too. The way these vines have run up the fruit trees is wonderful. Some time afterwards we made a pergola from the house to the stable and put Japanese, American, and French vines upon it. The Virginian Creepers, which have little pads to their fingers with which they fix themselves, are brilliant in woodland. Merely by putting one or two of them at the base of a tree one may, in good soil, get a noble flame of colour in autumn, and without doing harm to anything.

The greatest improvement of our day for the climber-lover is the pergola, so common in Italy and Southern France. In our country we have the advantage of being able to grow on it a greater number of climbers than the Italians could in their hot sun. Growing such plants on walls involves pruning, and much work that is anything but pretty, but with the pergola we can allow the plants their freedom, and there is the advantage of being able to see all round, under, and over them.

Many people have tried to form pergolas with deplorable results. People who should know better make pergolas with battens of Pine, Spruce, and rustic work, which begin to rot soon after they are put in. Fooling about with sap-wood simply means waste of time and means.

A pergola should be a want. To make it for the sake of making it is sure to end badly. Having fixed on a good position, the next thing is to give it good legs to stand on. No wooden supports, even the best, are much use. Some old stubs will last a long time, but they are not nearly as good as the old way of brick and stone. If it is to be heavily laden with climbers, a pergola must be well supported. A 14-inch brick pillar makes the best support, or one of stone. It is not enough to have strong pillars—they must be braced together; that is, the timbers must cross from one side to the other, and from one pillar to another. For the smaller timbers much will depend on the weight the pergola has to carry, but generally a simple and strong way of fixing is the best. Close rectangular trellising never looks well, and it will not last. The best way is that of the old French and English of using oak and chestnut battens fixed not too closely, or according to a definite plan, as in the modern Frenchman's garden.

We have tried every form of Bamboo and cane, and the effect at first was good, but in the end it did not do half as well as native Oak and Chestnut. There may be some more enduring tropical wood, but for the present we keep to these native woods. To show the need of bracing the pillars, I may say that when I made the garden of the crematorium at Golders Green, it was decided to have a bold pergola. The manager, with praiseworthy economy in starting a new affair, insisted on using old disfigured trees that had been cut down about the place, and the result was that one wild February day the whole thing was blown over. The pillars ought to have been braced both ways by stout squared timbers of Chestnut, Oak, or Larch.

The Ivy takes care of itself in the woods and copses, and though some people are careful to cut it off trees, it is a mistake to do so. One may do it when it overpowers a favourite or rare tree, but generally in woodland work it is best to let the Ivy alone for the sake of its beauty and to shelter wrens and other small birds. I rather like taking one of the fine forms of Ivy and putting it at the base of a tree, with a stone over it, leaving it to climb up.

To show how one may go to work, I may say that we are now planting groups of Hollies, the noblest of all evergreen shrubs, and when we plant a Holly we put a delicate climber against it, a Clematis, or the Flame Nasturtium, as the case may be. Some climbers are so fragile that they do not injure any shrub; if it does, it can be cut away. Wild roses may also be beautifully treated in a natural way, such as our own Dog rose or the Japanese ramblers people are so fond of. One can only see their highest beauty when they are running over or falling about a tree. Some climbers, too, that become weeds in rich garden soil, may be used with good effect to clothe fences. We have used the Hungarian Bindweed in that way; it is a handsome plant, but whilst in the garden it ruins everything else, on an orchard fence it is never in the way.

W. R.

CHAPTER I

CLIMBING PLANTS IN GARDENS AND IN NATURE

PLANTS of climbing habit occupy an important position among those cultivated by man, either for use or for ornament. It may be said of one of them, the grape vine, that it is God's most generous gift to mankind. The records of its cultivation and of the making of wine in Egypt go back five or six thousand years. And the vine is as beautiful as it is useful, for although it has failed to find a great deal of favour in this country as an ornamental shrub, this is due to our practice of valuing a plant either for its economic properties or for its decorative character. It can be useful or ornamental, not both. For this reason when considering climbing plants for the purposes of this volume we exclude those that are not used decoratively. The Cucumber, Tomato, Melon, Sweet Potato, Pepper, Pea, Vegetable Marrow, and Pumpkin will not for this reason come under notice here, although they are all climbers of great importance to man as food plants.

Our gardens owe much of their charm to plants of climbing habit. If we fail to make the best use of some of them it is either because we have not discovered their good qualities or we do not treat them in a way that enables them to display their habit to the best advantage. The curse of many climbers is the gardeners' method of "training" them. Examples of the worst kind are the

Allamanda, Dipladenia, Bougainvillea, Passiflora, and even the Rose and Clematis so often twisted and tied down in the form of a balloon! Could anything be less artistic, more unnatural, more wanting in feeling for a plant's character than this? The practice began in greenhouses, and was probably considered necessary for purposes of exhibition, and although we see much less of it now, it has not been entirely discarded. Out of doors there can be no excuse for this sort of cruelty. There, at any rate, climbing plants may be allowed space for the proper display of their natural habit, always with a due regard to what is best, not worst in nature's ways. Many plants that are trimmed, nailed or tied down would be much more effective if they were allowed greater freedom. This is true of all climbers. A little thought, a little inquiry as to what the plant likes and what is its natural habit would save our gardens from many ugly features and thus increase their charm.

I have learnt from experience that it is worse than useless to recommend in books on horticulture plants that are not generally known and are not likely to find their way into popular cultivation. At Kew one sees a considerable number of plants that deserve to be generally grown, but they haven't "caught on" with what I may call the gardening set, and they remain undiscovered by horticulture, though their day may yet come. I recollect that *Asparagus plumosus* was an inhabitant of the Succulent House at Kew for many years before it was discovered by someone and its value brought to the public notice, and there are not many more useful climbers to-day than this plant. The climbers described and recommended in this book therefore are those that are known by the well-informed gardener to be good plants. One hundred genera have been selected, and the species of each that may legitimately claim to be of proved horticultural merit enumerated. Anyone wishing to find out what plants would be most suitable, either for the outdoor garden, the greenhouse, or the stove, had better first read the chapter dealing with the special department, and then turn to Chapter XV for particulars of the plants recommended for it.

There are no doubt good plants which are not included in this list. In a book of this kind we must be selective, and strive as we may, there will be defects of commission and omission. Still, most requirements ought to be met in one hundred genera, and, at the price, if I may be allowed to say so, the book is comprehensive enough. The best one can hope for in a book such as the present is a safe indication, a helpful hint. To the man who means business and who has resourcefulness this will be sufficient. Those who want to be told everything must try an encyclopaedia.

Before dealing with climbers in their purely horticultural bearing it may be worth while to say something about them as they occur in nature, and to briefly set out what a climber is, and by what methods it is enabled to hold its own among plants that are self-supporting.

The embraces of some climbers are of such a character as to strangle the trees supporting them. Ivy has had that kind of effect on trees in certain circumstances, but its embrace is nothing when compared with that of some members of the fig tribe, gigantic Leguminosae and species of Clusia. They gradually wind themselves serpent-like round the trunks of trees, and as they tighten by reason of the growth of the host, the climbers interfere with the conduction of sap until finally the supporting tree is killed outright. It may be that in the struggle for existence this character has been developed in plants with thin stems to enable them to fight successfully for "a place in the sun." Without it they would stand a poor chance against umbrageous forest trees. "Sometimes one finds the hard basal parts of a liane (climber) twisted and coiled apparently round nothing. This is due to the fact that the original support has been killed, and then slowly rotting, has been denuded away by the wind and rain. Thus, many a liane of the tropical forest seems to have made use, when young, of some living plant with fairly thick erect stem as its first support, up which it has climbed into the crowns of higher trees" (Kerner). Sometimes the climber gets the worst of it, the encircled tree expanding until the pull on the coils is so great that the climber is killed.

Darwin in his *Movements of Plants* shows how all the growing parts of plants are continually circumnutating, and that climbers, when growing, do this very markedly, the end of the shoot in twiners and the tendrils or leaves in those which have special holdfasts to enable them to climb, describing quite wide circles in their efforts to catch on to some support. Tendril-bearing plants are much less aggressive than twiners in their struggles to climb upwards. Tendrils are very sensitive, and are so constructed that they can grasp and in a short time hold fast to a twig or other body that may afford support. Before this happens the tendril is straight, but afterwards it contracts itself spirally in the most beautiful manner, thus forming an elastic spring which gives a little to pressure from wind or to the weight of the shoot of which it is a part. Plants with the tendril method of climbing have an advantage over twiners, and this accounts for their being more numerous in nature.

Climbing plants have been divided into groups according to their particular habit of clinging. Thus there are (1) *Twiners*, which attach themselves to supports by twisting spirally around them. Examples are the Honeysuckle, Hop, and Scarlet Runner. The stoutest of tropical climbers belong to this group. (2) *Weavers*. These have slender stems which elongate and push their way among the branches of other plants before developing leaves and lateral shoots, by means of which they hold on. Some of them have spines or prickles which also help them to cling. Examples of this group are species of Rose, Honeysuckle, Asparagus, and Jasminum. (3) *Lattice Formers*. Plants which lean and build themselves up against a support without actually clinging to it. Some of the Cotoneasters, Euonymus, Allamanda, and some Fuchsias are examples of plants with this habit. (4) *Tendril Bearers*. A tendril may be a modification of a leaf, leaf stalk, leaflet, midrib, stipule, branchlet or flower stalk. At first very delicate and motile, it often becomes hard and strong almost as steel. Tendrils loop themselves round a support as though they possessed intelligence, and until they come in contact with one, they move about in a manner suggestive of the antennae of some insect. A great variety of plants are tendril bearers. Some of the most familiar are the Vine, Passion flower, Nepenthes, Gloriosa, Cucurbits, Pea and Clematis. Ampelopsis and some of the species of Vitis and Cissus form adhesive discs at the ends of their tendrils, by means of which they fasten themselves firmly with a kind of gum secreted by the disc, which hardens quickly. (5) *Root-*

ing Stems. The Ivy, Tecoma, Marcgravia, Philodendron, and other Aroids, some species of Cereus, *Ficus repens*, and other species of Ficus are examples of this group. The climbing roots of Ivy are only fixers, and do not absorb food unless they come in contact with soil, when they may change their function and perform that of ordinary roots. Thus Ivy growing on the ground has what may be termed feeding roots all along its stem.

CHAPTER II

HARDY CLIMBERS

THE charm of English gardens is very largely due to the artistic employment of a variety of plants which are either climbers by nature or made to serve the purpose of climbers by the application of a little art. If we were limited strictly to plants of climbing habit for the decoration of buildings and other objects, we should lose the effect of the trained shrub and tree. The beauty of a well-trained Pear, Cherry, Plum, Pyracantha, Ceanothus, Cotoneaster, Escallonia, Edwardsia, Euonymus, and Forsythia is generally recognised, yet not one of these is strictly a climber. Even *Magnolia grandiflora*, *Eriobotrya japonica*, *Prunus triloba*, and *Cydonia japonica* are used most effectively for clothing walls. It is surprising what the resourceful cultivator can do in the way of adapting plants to his purposes by the judicious use of the knife and the wall nail. There are few more lovely objects than a peach, cherry, or plum-covered wall in the flowering season. One of the college buildings at Cambridge is, or used to be, almost entirely covered with Tamarix, a glorious object at all times, and especially so when in flower. The Camellia when trained flat against the wall is both effective and happy. Sir Joseph Paxton used it largely in this way, and it is common enough grown against a wall in the south of England.

From what has been said it will be evident that there are many free-growing shrubs, and a considerable number of what are known as trees that may be turned to account in the furnishing of walls and fences. Good use is sometimes made of the wall for the double purpose of affording a certain amount of protection and giving support to shrubs that are too tender to bear a more open position. The walls at Kew and in other gardens where large collections are grown are wholly employed for this purpose. Quite a long list of tender shrubs which are happy when grown close to a wall might be given from the Kew experience alone. The purpose of this book, however, is not so much to show how many plants there are that could be grown against walls, with advantage to the plants themselves, as to point out the best of those which have been successfully cultivated in this manner.

The most useful climber in the world is the Ivy, a strong statement perhaps, but one which few Englishmen would gainsay. It will make the ugliest of buildings picturesque, it will clothe old tree trunks, cover walls and fences, and form picturesque pillars at comparatively little cost; it will furnish the ground as no other shrub can; it will grow in conditions where few other plants will live; and as for soil, almost any kind will satisfy the Ivy—indeed, it will grow where there is scarcely any soil at all. "A rare old plant is the Ivy green." There are so many varieties, hundreds of them according to some authorities, all developed from the common *Hedera Helix*, a native of Europe, North Africa, and West Asia. Its garden history will be found in another part of this book.

Next in value to the Ivy we should place *Ampelopsis Veitchii*, a plant with many names, which need not trouble us here, except to mention that its name in botanical works is *Vitis inconstans*. Like the Ivy it can be used to cover a multitude of sins of the architect and gardener. Like the Ivy, too, it is very good-natured, as the townsman well knows. Among the many plants that we owe to Japan it is doubtful whether there is one which has proved such a blessing as this little clinging vine.

Wistaria chinensis (see Plates II and III) is a noble climber, unquestionably the most beautiful we possess as a flowering plant. It is not as much used as it deserves to be, probably owing to its requirements being somewhat exacting, for its shoots must be trained and pruned regularly to keep it in order. It loves sunshine, in fact will not thrive unless it gets plenty, and it behaves as if it would live for ever when planted at the foot of a south wall where there is ample room for its shoots to extend. In this respect it resembles the Vine (*Vitis vinifera*), another noble climber, whose merits as a decorative plant gardeners overlook. Because it does not behave well in the open air as a fruit-producer, the vine appears to have fallen into discredit as a decorative plant. Here and there one sees it flourishing, generally in old gardens, clinging to buildings, or clothing a summer-house, and it is also to be seen in a few places scrambling over trees, where its summer effect is most picturesque. Many species of Vitis have lately been imported from China, some of which are certain to become favourites when they

Plate III. STEM OF WISTARIA IN THE CONSERVATORY AT SYSTON HALL

PLATE II

WISTARIA CHINENSIS

are better known. There is a collection of them on a pergola at Kew, where their characters may be studied with advantage.

Clematis occupies a leading place among our best outdoor climbing plants. Everyone loves our native Traveller's Joy (*Clematis Vitalba*), yet it is not as frequently seen in the garden and park as it deserves to be, for it does not interfere materially with the tree or shrub to which it clings for support, and it might be seen much more frequently in the woodland. It must have plenty of sunshine, and, of course it likes lime, as all Clematises do. There is the lovely *C. montana* with its several varieties, and for gardens in the south the New Zealand *C. indivisa* might be turned to good account. The larger flowered species and garden forms, of which *C. Jackmanii* is a typical example, have not yet found the place in open-air gardening for which they are eminently fitted. We see them as balloon-trained specimens at our exhibitions, and following the lead of the trade exhibitors we attempt their cultivation only as pot plants, with the exception of places that might be counted on one's fingers, where the large-flowered red Clematises are afforded generous treatment as wall climbers.

Rose, Honeysuckle and Jasmine, these are the climbers whose praises are sung by poets and whose charms are portrayed by artists, for they play a large part in the beautifying of the English garden, from the cottager's small enclosure to the most spacious domain. Honeysuckle and Jasmine are beloved because of their fragrance; they are not very showy in flower, yet they are always a delight, particularly when they receive a little attention from the cultivator, Honeysuckles especially being responsive to good treatment.

A most useful plant is the Winter Jasmine (*J. nudiflorum*), which bursts into bloom in December. We owe it, as we do so many good things, to Japan. It always looks its best when against a wall, probably because of the shelter from wind that it gets in such a position. Its Chinese sister, *J. primulinum*, has not yet distinguished itself in English gardens, appearing to be too tender to be grown outside, in the neighbourhood of London at any rate, though we have seen it flowering nicely in a sheltered position against a south wall in November. Properly it ought not to be classed as a climber, though it is pretty certain to be treated as one in English gardens. The great Burmese Honeysuckle (*Lonicera Hildebrandtiana*), although a magnificent climber in its mountain home, has yet to prove its usefulness in this country. In the greenhouse it is a straggler, and not free with blossom. Mr. Veitch grows and flowers it well in his Exeter nursery, and it has done fairly well out-of-doors here and there in Cornwall and in South-west Ireland; possibly if some clever breeder would exercise his art in crossing honeysuckles he would produce hybrids combining the vigour of say *L. etrusca* and *L. Hildebrandii* with the floral qualities of our native species and the North American *L. sempervirens*.

Roses must have a chapter to themselves. After all, when we begin to talk about beautiful hardy climbers, one is certain to begin with "Well, there are Roses." And there *are* Roses nowadays, climbers such as our grandfathers never dreamt of, thanks in the first place to the introduction of *R. Wichuraiana* and Crimson Rambler, and in the second place to the success of the breeder who has combined the qualities of these two with so many of our other garden roses. There were, of course, numerous beauti-

PLATE IV. CHINESE BRAMBLES

Rubus coreanus, R. thibetanus, R. corchorifolius

ful roses of scandent habit fifty years ago, memories of them as seen clothing cottages in country places in England are cherished by most people. They were of the type of Flora, Ruga, Dundee Rambler and Félicité Perpétue, and they are among the best of what are popularly known as rambler or pergola Roses to-day. No more need be said here of the qualities and uses of climbing Roses. Their relations the Brambles (Rubus) have jumped the garden fence owing to the introduction from China of a number of promising climbing species (see Plates IV and V). There is a good collection of them near the Pagoda at Kew, and some appear to have qualities which should prove attractive horticulturally. Distinctly climbing in habit, they have a wide range of leaf variation, and as they appear to be quite hardy there should be no difficulty in proving their worth. Messrs. J. Veitch & Sons, who introduced most of them through their collector Mr. Wilson, believed in them, for they exhibited collections of them periodically at the shows.

A useful climber, whose merits have been overlooked, is *Hydrangea scandens;* it clings like Ivy, and has bright green, heart-shaped leaves, which are deciduous. The flowers are not of much account; indeed, they are rarely produced. It has decided merit as a wall climber, as it covers a large area in a comparatively short time, and is quite hardy.

The claims of certain annuals as climbers must not be overlooked. The Scarlet Runner Bean, though considered too vulgar by some people for a place among decorative plants, is as beautiful as it is useful. The climbing Tropæolums are general favourites. They are capable of doing a great deal in a short time towards blotting out unsightly objects, and they are in themselves full of attractions. It is surprising what can be done in this way with the aid of a threepenny packet of seeds and a little imagination. The Canary Creeper (*T. aduncum*) is of the same quality, except that it has small flowers and is less robust. This is the place to call attention to the claims of *T. speciosum*, the pride of some gardeners, the despair of others. *T. pentaphyllum* and *T. tuberosum* also are not without attractions. The three last-named species are, of course, perennial, though their stems are annual. If there is one annual climber which has received the full share of popular favour it is the Sweet Pea (*Lathyrus odoratus*), but the beautiful perennial species of the genus might well be more in evidence in gardens in every class. Calystegia, Convolvulus, some of the gourds (see separate chapter), and Lophospermum deserve to be included here. The merits of the Hop also should not be overlooked. Gardeners are too ready to relegate to a back place or pitch out altogether plants whose associations are not strictly horticultural. The Japanese Hop (*Humulus japonicus*) is a quick growing annual with handsome foliage and large panicles of feathery flowers, which have a rather unpleasant odour. It likes a sunny position, and if the seeds are sown in April it will romp away.

A list of the genera which furnish the best hardy climbers is here given. For particulars as to species and treatment the descriptive list given under Chapter XV should be consulted.

Abelia.
Aconitum.
Actinidia.
Akebia.
Ampelopsis.
Aristolochia.
Berberidopsis.
Bignonia.
Boussingaultia.
Calystegia.

PLATE V. CHINESE BRAMBLES

R. omeiensis, and R. biflorus var. quinqueflorus

Celastrus.
Clematis.
Convolvulus.
Eccremocarpus.
Ercilla.
Fuchsia.
Hedera.
Humulus.
Hydrangea.
Ipomœa.
Jasminum.
Kadsura.
Lardizabala.
Lathyrus.
Lonicera.
Lycium.
Maurandia.
Menispermum.
Muehlenbeckia.
Mutisia.
Passiflora.
Periploca.
Phaseolus.
Polygonum.
Rhus.
Rhyncospermum.
Rosa.
Rubus.
Schizandra.
Smilax.
Solanum.
Stauntonia.
Tecoma.
Tropæolum.
Vitis.
Wistaria.

EVERGREEN SHRUBS FOR WALLS

Boundary walls are often necessary, but no one likes to see a naked wall. It is therefore usual to hide them either by covering them with Ivy or planting a line of shrubs or trees in front of them. There is another, and in some situations a more appropriate way, and this is by covering them with a selection of evergreen shrubs. Ivy is good, but it is common. There are walls on which no evergreen except Ivy would thrive; for them Ivy must be used.

Where there is light and air, assuming of course that the wall is not wanted for the cultivation of fruit, and that deciduous plants would not do, as the wall would be practically bare in winter, then evergreen shrubs should be used. There are plenty of them, so that a collection might be indulged in, especially if the wall is in a conspicuous place.

There are walls of this kind in the Royal Gardens, Kew. They were formerly boundary walls, and they have been utilised for shrubs that required protection, many not being climbers. They have become quite an interesting feature of the place. Some are deciduous, and for our present purpose they need not be considered. A list of the evergreens only is given here. With few exceptions they are plants which are not sufficiently hardy to grow permanently in the open in this country except in such counties as Devon and Cornwall. Even with the protection afforded them at Kew by the wall which supports them they sometimes get frostbitten. Some have been in their present position for at least fifty years. They are not nailed flat against the wall, the main branches only being fixed, the others only shortened when necessary. Thus treated, many of them have formed a perfect screen of foliage a foot or more through, completely hiding the wall and at the same time presenting a pleasing, even decorative, front.

The treatment may possibly be called mutilation, a misuse of plants which cannot do themselves justice when nailed against a wall and kept more or less cropped. It is pardonable, however, in such conditions as are described above. If the plants were not grown in this way they couldn't be grown at all. Needs must when the climate drives! It is not pretended that the appended list includes all evergreen shrubs that may be successfully used as wall screens, but the selection is considered sufficiently embracing for most gardens.

EVERGREEN SHRUBS FOR WALLS

Adenocarpus decorticans, Spain
„ foliolosus, Canaries
Anthyllis Hermanniae, S. Europe
Aristotelia Macqui, Chili
Azara microphylla, Chili
Bupleurum fruticosum, Medit.
Camellia, Japan
Ceanothus, N. America
Choisya ternata, Mexico
Convolvulus Cneorum, S. Europe
Corokia Cotoneaster, New Zealand
Cotoneaster, India and China
Crataegus. *See* Pyracantha
Discaria longispina, Chili
Edwardsia. *See* Sophora
Eriobotrya japonica, Japan
Escallonia, S. America
Euonymus radicans, Japan
Fabiana imbricata, Chili
Feijoa Sellowiana, Brazil
Garrya elliptica, California
„ macrophylla, Mexico
„ Thurettii, Garden hybrid
Griselinia littoralis, New Zealand
Jasminum humile, Himalaya
„ primulinum, China
Leptospermum laevigatum, Australia
Ligustrum Henryi, China
Lonicera Henryi, China
Magnolia Delavayi, China
„ grandiflora, U.S.A.
Myrsine africana, Himalaya, &c.
Myrtus communis, Medit.
„ „ tarentina
Olea europaea, Asia Minor
Olearia macrodonta, N. Zealand
Osteomeles anthyllidifolia, China
„ Schwerinii, China
„ subrotunda, China
Pittosporum Ralphii, N. Zealand
„ crassifolium, New Zealand
Pyracantha angustifolia, China
„ coccinea, S. Europe
„ crenulata, Himalaya
Rhaphithamnus cyanocarpus, Chili
Schinus Bonplandianus, Brazil
Sophora tetraptera, New Zealand
„ „ var. microphylla
Stranvaesia undulata, China
Trachelospermum jasminoides, Japan
Tricuspidaria dependens, Chili
Umbellularia californica, California
Viburnum macrocephalum, China
„ rhytidophyllum, China

CHAPTER III

GREENHOUSE CLIMBERS

A LARGE number of plants of strictly climbing habit, and many others which are not climbers, but are made to serve that purpose, are grown for the decoration of spacious greenhouses and conservatories. They could not well be grown so as to display their attractions of leaf and flower unless they had the support of pillars or strained wires near the rafters (see Plate XI) which fortunately provide generally suitable conditions of light and air, and at the same time afford easy means of screening with greenery more or less unsightly features. It is worth while to grow some climbers in tall greenhouses even though they do not flower. Such large structures as the Palm House and the Temperate House at Kew would have an unfurnished appearance were it not for the climbers which are freely used to drape pillar, gallery, and rafter. In smaller houses there is little or no need to use climbers for the purposes mentioned, but as a number of these plants can be really well grown only in small houses, their cultivation is practised to a considerable extent solely for the sake of the plants themselves. At the same time, no good grower of orchids would have climbers over his plants, as they interfere with the regulation of sunlight and air in the house, and they often harbour insects and other pests.

The best of all structures for the display of plants of climbing habit is the corridor greenhouse, usually a long, lofty, narrow structure connecting a group of greenhouses or potting sheds. Corridors were a feature of importance in the old South Kensington Garden, and at Chatsworth they are still important because of their extent and the large variety of climbers they contain. The Chatsworth corridors were copied at the Crystal Palace by Sir Joseph Paxton, and forty years ago these also contained an interesting collection of greenhouse climbers. In the Botanic Gardens at Edinburgh and at Cambridge there are large corridors, richly furnished with climbers. The late Mr. Joseph Chamberlain was justly proud of the corridor which connected his house with his orchid and other greenhouses at Highbury. It had a tiled floor, was lit by electricity, whilst climbing plants on each side, with hanging baskets overhead, furnished it. It was a delightful promenade in which those who wished could talk and smoke comfortably, whilst others interested in the contents of the plant houses could go their own way without a guide.

Climbers intended to cover a large area must be provided with plenty of root room. Just as grape vines are treated liberally with respect to soil, so all strong growing climbers must have proper provision for root extension. Fortunately many of them are able to forage on their own account, for it is not unusual to find roots intended to occupy a small amount of space growing out under stages and into paths, and even through the outside walls to the soil beyond. Plants that succeed in doing this are almost capable of looking after themselves. At the same time proper borders should be made in which the drainage and soil are sufficient to provide what the plant requires, and to keep it healthy. In corridors where the floor is tiled or flagged a border 2 feet wide should be made. As far as the welfare of the plants can be considered the floor had better be soil covered with a layer of fine gravel, but that is a detail which circumstances must decide. Where the floor is tiled the border should be raised above the floor level and kept in position with upright tiles or other edging. This serves to prevent water running from the paths into the borders. The soil for the border must be good in quality, and although certain plants require a particular kind of soil, Lapageria and Dipladenia for example must have pure peat—generally a mixture of good turfy loam, leaf mould, and coarse sand suits greenhouse climbers. Peat is not recommended to be mixed with other soils, because in a border it is apt to become sour and cause mischief.

In most conservatories and greenhouses root accommodation can be provided under the side stages or at the foot of pillars, where the border should be made as recommended. Failing this, boxes or large pots have to be used. For some climbers it is an advantage to have the roots quite under control, and for this reason pot or box is preferable for them. They can be specially fed, or for the purpose of resting or checking growth water can be withheld for a time. These large root receptacles are unfortunately unsightly, still they can be utilised for trailing plants, which serve to hide them.

When climbers are to be grown in pots standing on the stages in small houses their treatment must be, to some extent at any rate, the same as that given to the occupants of the house generally. They will require training and keeping within bounds, the treatment that is best in such a position being the restricted or short spur system as practised for grape vines. They then flower better, and are less likely to outgrow their space.

Climbers are always most effective when their stems are allowed to grow with a certain amount of freedom. A tangle of shoots is natural, and if they are flowering plants their flowers produce a more pleasing effect than when strict training is practised.

A list of climbing plants for cultivation in greenhouses, corridors and conservatories, limited strictly to plants of climbing habit, would exclude a number of shrubs which are grown as climbers. It has already been pointed out that it is difficult to draw the line between shrubs that are climbers and those that are not, and for our purpose it is not necessary to draw it. The following plants are known to be suitable for the purposes named. It is only necessary to mention the genera here. The alphabetical list under Chapter XIV should be consulted as to species :—

Abutilon (see Plate XIV).
Acacia.
Asparagus.
Bignonia.
Bomarea.
Bougainvillea.
Cassia.
Clematis.
Clianthus.
Cobaea.
Fuchsia.
Habrothamnus (Cestrum).
Hibbertia.
Hidalgoa.
Ipomœa.
Kennedya.
Lapageria.
Lathyrus.
Lonicera.
Mandevilla.
Passiflora.
Pereskia.
Plumbago.
Rhodochiton.
Rosa.
Rubus.
Ruscus.
Senecio.
Solanum.
Stauntonia.
Tacsonia.
Tecoma.
Thunbergia.

CHAPTER IV

STOVE CLIMBERS

HORTICULTURALLY the only difference between climbers for the greenhouse and climbers for the stove is one of temperature. Large tropical houses are not numerous in this country, for the very good reason that they are costly to maintain, and as the means necessary to provide the required temperature have to be mainly artificial, plants so cultivated are rarely happy. The conditions in nature are very different from those provided by hot water pipes and a liberal use of the hosepipe and syringe. Most important of all, direct sunlight is too often wanting for the successful cultivation of plants which in nature are generally exposed to bright sunshine. Climbers have developed the habit of struggling upwards in the effort to grow beyond the canopy of foliage of the trees which shut out the direct sunlight. They require an abundance of light and air for their proper development, and for the production of flowers and fruits. It is for this reason that climbers from distant tropical regions do not flower in cultivation with us satisfactorily; they miss the sunshine and air which they get on the roof of the forest in the tropics. Such plants as the Bauhinia, *Camoensia maxima*, *Hodgsonia heteroclita*, Hexacentris, and some of the Aristolochias are of this character. At the same time there are many tropical climbers which can be successfully grown in plant houses.

In these days stove plants are less popular than they

were half a century or less ago, and there is no getting away from the fact that a tropical plant house is often so hot and moist that the plants in it can only be inspected in more or less discomfort. Nevertheless there are still among us horticulturists who love to cultivate plants from tropical countries, many of which are climbers of great beauty and charm. It would not be difficult to build a glass house specially adapted for the cultivation of tropical climbers. Such a house should be constructed so as to admit the maximum amount of sunshine, the borders heated from below, and the air warmed by means of hot water pipes fixed near the roof.

A serious defect in all our artificially heated plant houses is that the heat comes from below, and in tropical houses in winter this is injurious to plants. One of the most striking examples of what is meant is the Palm House at Kew, the roof of which is iron and glass and the floor open-iron grating, below which are many rows of hot water pipes. To maintain the required temperature in winter these pipes have to be kept hot, and the effect of the heated dry air rising from below and impinging against the delicate under surface of the leaves is harmful to most plants. Climbers, which are necessarily near the roof, do not suffer so much as the plants lower down, but even they would be happier if the conditions with respect to temperature were better.

A list of climbers suitable for a tropical house might include some of the plants mentioned in the list for a greenhouse. Many plants are fairly adaptive with respect to temperature. *Vitis vinifera*, for example, which may be grown in the open air in England, and is also quite happy under ultratropical treatment; the common Passion flower

Passiflora coerulea grows flowers and fruits against a south wall in England, yet it is also quite happy in the greenhouse and conservatory, and is nowhere more successful than in a tropical house. *Solanum Wendlandii* grew and flowered well out of doors in the garden of the late Sir Trevor Lawrence at Burford, and it is now fairly common as a greenhouse plant, yet it is a native of the tropical forests of Brazil, and it has never been seen anywhere in greater luxuriance than in the hot, moist Water Lily House at Kew.

At the same time many tropical plants will not thrive in other than a stove temperature. The following list of genera is an attempt at a selection of climbers which require a tropical climate and which are known to be cultivated in the gardens of this country as ornamental plants:—

Allamanda.
Aristolochia.
Beaumontia.
Bignonia.
Cereus.
Clerodendron.
Clitoria.
Combretum.
Dioscorea.
Dipladenia.
Gloriosa.
Hoya.
Marcgravia.
Monstera.
Mucuna.
Odontadenia.
Oxera.
Passiflora.
Petraea.
Philodendron.
Pothos.
Selaginella.
Smilax.
Solandra.
Stephanotis.
Strophanthus.
Thunbergia.

CHAPTER V

CONSTRUCTION OF PERGOLAS

A PERGOLA has come to be looked upon as a necessary feature in a good class garden. As a support for climbing plants it has many advantages, and for that reason its usefulness must be considered in a book about climbers. At the same time one cannot overlook the fact that in some gardens the pergola is an eyesore, and that some pergolas which one sees would be an eyesore anywhere. Italy, where the pergola, a kind of balcony or arbour, had its origin, is a land of sunshine, where coolness and shade are desirable for the greater portion of the year. There is much less need for them in the gardens of these islands, where a balcony against the house, a well-placed summer-house, a group of trees with spreading branches, or even one of the spreading chestnut tree pattern afford shade and shelter, and are more appropriate.

But we have adapted the pergola to another purpose, namely, as a more or less ornamental feature in itself, climbing plants being trained over it as a kind of excuse for its being there. In this respect the pergola is no worse than the great majority of other structures that are allowed in the garden. Some, such as the greenhouse and the shelter or summer-house, are tolerable because they have a definite use. But many gardens are spoilt by silly attempts to add variety by the introduction of what are supposed to be works of art in the shape of temples, statues, well-heads, sundials, elaborately designed seats, fountains, summer-houses that are not inviting, and pergolas. My advice therefore to those who are worried by a pergola that has become troublesome is, sweep it away and plant trees or shrubs in its place; and to those who feel inclined to build one I would say, think twice and thrice before deciding. A pergola in the wrong place is distressing; an ugly pergola is a sin against art; a well placed pergola of good design, suitable for climbing plants, may be a delightful feature and a source of interest during summer; but it will not be cheap, and it will need a lot of attention from the gardener; it must be well furnished with the right kind of plants. There are such pergolas in England, but not many.

The most pergolarised garden I have seen is that formed by the late Lord Battersea, at Overstrand, near Cromer. Most of the walks appeared to be roofed with pergolas, on which grew a great variety of climbers. In summer the plants were both attractive and interesting, so much so that one did not notice the effect of the pergolas in the general scheme. Probably in winter they would give the garden a kind of bird-cage look.

There are sometimes positions in a garden where a pergola would not be unsuitable. The best is as a covering to a walk from the house to a shelter house or other structure; or to an entrance gate. Even then it must be considered from several standpoints, for it sometimes happens that a pergola has been erected where it destroys the best view in the garden. Another likely position is over a path running parallel to a tall hedge, the latter to form one side of the pergola, as it were. It must not be forgotten that the plants trained up and over a heavy-topped pergola cannot be properly seen from the inside. There are pergolas whose roofs have become a thick tangle of climbers which seen from inside is a mere thatch of stems and leaves, all their charms being displayed above outside, where only the birds can enjoy them.

No heavy form of pergola can look well in a garden in this country. At any rate, I have never seen one that I would not have removed had it been mine. The lighter they are in construction the better. Larch and other poles are recommended, and some designs for them are simply treillage arranged pergolawise. The objection to wood is that if used in any thickness it has a heavy look, and if made of light material it does not last long. There is nothing like iron for lightness in effect, and durability. Gas piping 1½-inch in diameter is excellent for the standards or pillars, and they can be kept in position at the top by an iron rod ½-inch in diameter, turned at each end so as to hook into the upright pipes. These rods can be either straight or curved to taste. Thus a number of iron arches spanning the path are formed, and they can be connected at the sides by fixing rods along the top of the standards. The plants are trained on these so as to form a series of arches, and there is no danger of a tangle of shoots overhead; moreover the plants can be easily seen from the path, and they get room and the maximum of light. There are two pergolas of this kind at Kew, one near the rock garden, devoted to roses, another, near the pagoda, on which a collection of hardy species of Vitis and the Wistarias are trained. For the greater part of the year these two pergolas are unattractive, one may say they are downright ugly throughout the winter. Indeed I have never seen a pergola in winter in this country that wasn't.

How to make a pergola and keep it from becoming dull and irritating at any time is a question which has yet to be answered. By clothing it with evergreen climbers one might make it passable in winter, but it would never have a gay time, would be a dull object always. A mixture of rose, clematis, honeysuckle, and evergreen might be managed, but it would be difficult to keep in balance. The choice of plants would depend on space and situation, and there is great variety to select from. A pergola devoted entirely to Wistaria would be magnificent when the plants were in bloom. The rose pergola at Kew is a beautiful sight in June, when most of the plants, all of the Rambler type, are in full blow. The grape vine would be an excellent plant to use in this way, and in sunny localities it might be fairly fruitful.

From what has been said it will be seen that I do not recommend the pergola except solely as a structure for the accommodation of climbing plants. As a purely architectural feature in the garden I have no patience with it. The plashed alleys of the sixteenth-century gardens served the purpose at least as well, and were less unsightly in winter. I may be wrong, but I certainly am a heretic in this question of architectural art in the garden. To me a block of stone of fantastic form with a sundial on it is affectation—make-believe. Naked human figures in stone stuck about in the garden should either be covered or taken indoors in cold weather; when I see them I feel disposed to offer them a muffler, an umbrella, or a Burberry. The unattractive seats in stone that are becoming fashionable must be meant for the ladies whose Sandow clothing does not admit of sitting down. Surely, the garden should be comfortable, peaceful, beautiful without affectation's artful aid, made so by plant, leaf, and flower, all after nature's best, healthy and pleasant to look at.

CHAPTER VI

CLIMBERS FOR VERANDAHS, HOUSE WALLS, AND ARBOURS

THE pergola is a sort of verandah-archway, and the objections that have been raised to it may be urged to some extent against other contrivances of the kind. Archways are not always suitably placed; they are sometimes ridiculous both in form and position, spanning a straight path midway between entrance gate and house for example, a common enough spot for one, yet as absurd as a door would be if placed there. An arch should suggest an entrance to somewhere; a change of scene; therefore the most happily placed arch in the garden is that spanning a gateway, or at the opening in a boundary fence separating say the pleasure from the kitchen garden. A well-built arch in such a position, clothed with a suitable climber, is good to look at. A bold stone archway as an entrance to a garden, with a climbing rose, clematis, or vine clinging to it, is better than any post or stone pillar. Climbers on arches must be allowed to grow with a certain amount of freedom, close cropping or training only spoils their effect. The ivy-clad entrance, although somewhat sad looking, is better than bare stone or wood. There is nothing to beat a good rose, one that makes long, strong shoots and flowers profusely.

The open-sided summer-house or arbour offers suitable support for hardy climbers; Tecoma, Clematis, Passiflora, Polygonum, and Wistaria for flowers, and Aristolochia, Humulus, Menispermum, and Vitis for foliage. Most roses are objectionable because of their thorns. The same selection will serve for the verandah, adding Forsythia, Jasminum, Berberidopsis, Lonicera, Fuchsia, and Calystegia, for their flowers and fitness of habit.

On the flat walls of houses and other buildings where some protection from cold is afforded there are more than enough suitable climbers for the many positions there provided. On walls facing south the sun-loving plants must be given preference, and in very sheltered places even tender plants, such as *Clianthus puniceus*, *Mutisia decurrens*, *Trachelospermum jasminoides*, and *Solanum Wendlandii*, *S. crispum*, and *S. jasminoides* may be tried. Ivy and *Ampelopsis Veitchii* are good enough for any position, and if climbers are required to cover walls in the quickest time, and with the minimum amount of attention, these are the plants to do it. If I were limited to the use of one climber for a wall, my choice would be this Ampelopsis. There remain the shrubs, such as Cotoneaster, Pyracantha, Ceanothus, Euonymus, Cydonia, and Edwardsia, all good wall plants requiring only a little shaping. They need to be nailed to the wall, as many of the true climbers do, unless wire supports are provided. Really good wall positions should not be lost sight of for pears, plums, and cherries. Many a gable end is turned to account by men who know what is needed to grow first-rate pears. These fruit-trees when in flower are a pleasing sight, and in the autumn when the fruit hangs thick on the branches they are still more pleasing. Roses on buildings are a common enough feature. They are dealt with in the chapter devoted to them in this book.

Cultural details for these hardy climbers will be found in the descriptive list (Chapter XV), but a few general directions may be given here. Most important of all is position. It isn't much use planting tender plants in exposed places, nor those that require plenty of sunshine in positions where they will not get it. Therefore, when making a selection attention should be paid to the needs of the plant with respect to exposure. As to soil, it pays to do these plants well from the first, and if borders do not already exist where the climbers are to be put, suitable borders should be made. It may be sufficient for each plant to take out a barrowful or so of soil, and to see that the drainage is all right before refilling the hole with a suitable compost. Some plants are not particular, will grow in anything that can be called soil; still one never knows what has been filled in at the foot of walls, and it is poor economy to risk it without making examination.

Pruning is an operation for which it is difficult to give directions of a general character. So much depends on the nature of the plant, its habit of growth and time of flowering; also on the position it occupies. As a rule hardy climbers require little pruning. Those grown for their flowers may have their shoots shortened soon after the flowers are over, but it will probably be necessary to examine them again in early spring. Evergreen climbers require no more pruning than is needed to keep them in position. Such plants as the grape vine, Passion flower, and Wistaria are best spur-pruned in winter.

CHAPTER VII

CLIMBERS ON TREES

It has already been shown that the natural support for a climbing plant is a tree or stout shrub. In nature climbers have nothing else to climb, except perhaps a rocky projection. There is, however, often a struggle for position, and the ill effects of some climbers, such as Ivy, on the host plant make it inadvisable to set climbers to grow over trees or shrubs that are themselves of value. No gardener who knows the habits of ivy allows it to fasten itself on a tree, unless it be one of no importance. Yet there are a few climbers which are not unkind to their hosts. Clematis, Tecoma, Roses, and Vines, which are not twiners, and therefore have not a tight and ever-tightening embrace, may be allowed to climb and hang themselves upon trees without danger.

In his book on *Hardy Trees and Shrubs*, Mr. W. J. Bean gives some useful hints on tree climbers. "The establishment of a climber in close enough proximity to a tree to enable it to overrun it requires some consideration. It is often of little use planting it at the base of the trunk. Although frequently selected, that spot is too dry and too shady, except in decrepit trees or trees with tall, bare trunks. If any branches come near enough to the ground to enable the newly planted climber to be attached to them, that is usually the best place to select. It may be necessary, however, to secure the branch against being blown about too roughly by storm, and so pulling out the climber with it. A stout post set in the ground may serve at once for the climber to grow up and to secure the branch to. The establishment of a climber on living trees and shrubs is also hampered and delayed by its having their active roots to contend with. A good plan in this case is to sink a tub or barrel, with the bottom knocked out, level with the surface of the soil, and fill it with rich soil, in which the climber is to be planted. This allows it to grow free from interference by other roots for a year or two and thus get firmly established. If the tube be of soft wood, it may be allowed to remain and decay."

In making a selection of climbers to be grown as above described, one must be guided by the position, size, and character of the garden, and the size and habit of the trees or shrubs to be used as hosts. The following are generally useful, being easy to establish and able to look after themselves pretty well.

Ampelopsis quinquefolia.
" Veitchii.
Aristolochia Sipho.
Celastrus articulatus.
Clematis calycina.
" Jackmanii.
" montana.
" Vitalba.
Humulus Lupulus.
Hydrangea scandens.
Lonicera etrusca.
" Hildebrandtiana.
" japonica.
Menispermum canadense.
Polygonum baldschuanicum.
Rosa Banksiana.
" gigantea.
" moschata.
Other climbing roses.
Solanum crispum.
" jasminoides (see Plate X).
Vitis Coignetiæ.
" Labrusca.
" vinifera.
Wistaria chinensis.
" multijuga.

CHAPTER VIII

CLIMBING ROSES

MANY species of Rosa are climbers, and gardeners have succeeded in adding to the number by crossing them with each other and with species that are not climbers. The king of climbing Roses is *R. gigantea*, a native of Upper Burma, and known as a garden plant in Europe for the last twenty-five years. So far it has resisted all attempts to raise a good hybrid from it, at any rate none has been recorded, and it has proved awkward in other ways. That it has qualities of a high order may be seen from the following account of it in Burma: "*Rosa gigantea* grows in profusion immediately opposite the window I am now writing at, and for a hundred yards or more away. The boles of some of the plants are as thick as a man's thigh. It is a creeper, and does not flower until it gets over or beyond the tree it climbs. These specimens are on large evergreen trees, and their roots are in limestone and vegetable mould, through which run springs of pure water. . . . The whole of a large group of trees on the southern and western side is covered up to fifty and eighty feet in height with the Roses, and when in full bloom they look like a sheet of white, and the air all round is deliciously scented. It is certainly a glorious sight." The flowers are six inches across and milk white. If only we could get Roses with this habit, and as free flowering as the best of our climbing garden sorts are, how useful they would be.

The most popular climbing Roses to-day are descendants from two wild species, namely *R. multiflora* and *R. Wichuraiana*, both natives of China and Japan, the former a true climber, the latter a trailer, with stems many feet long and shining evergreen leaves. Crimson Rambler, a variety of *R. multiflora*, set the fashion when it was introduced from Japan in 1893. It revealed the rose in a new character, or, at any rate, one which had not attracted much attention before, and the breeder set to work to raise more of the same type. They are with us now by the dozen, one might almost say hundred. Thanks to these loose-growing, free-flowering, easily-cultivated Rambler Roses, our gardens are now really rich in rose effects produced with the aid of the pergola, arch, pillar, and wall. If only *R. gigantea* could be induced to breed with some of them, but that may come.

Climbing decorative Roses are now a feature at flower shows; indeed, they enable Rose experts to make far more effective displays than were possible when specimen roses were ugly, formal things, quite unlike anything in nature, or yet in art worthy of the name. It is so much easier, too, to grow roses on natural lines, and the climbing trailing sorts are just what was needed to wean men from a liking for the severely-pruned, painfully-staked rose bush.

Mr. Pemberton says the Hybrid China Roses (*gallica* × *indica*), a production of the early part of the nineteenth century, were the pioneers of autumn flowering Roses: "What a sensation the advent of these, for the most part strong-growing, free-flowering pillar Roses, must have created. Nothing like them had been seen before. . . . Some few are with us still, and may they long continue. Amongst these is Blairii No. 2, raised by Mr. Blair in 1845, a most rampant grower, throwing out shoots ten or twelve feet long, and quickly covering wall or pillar. . . . It is frequently to be seen covering the front of old farmhouses, for it at one time obtained great popularity. Two other excellent examples of the Hybrid China are Mme. Plantier, pure white, sent out in 1835, and Fulgens, a brilliant crimson."

There are some useful climbing garden Roses among the Ayrshire group (*R. arvensis*), which are good-natured and free-flowering. Three of the best of these are Dundee Rambler, Bennett's Seedling, and Splendens. The so-called evergreen Roses are descendants of *R. sempervirens.* This species has long, slender, green shoots, armed with red prickles, and bearing shining green leaves, which remain fresh on the plant well into the winter. Félicité Perpétue is one of the best of its offspring.

There are climbing Hybrid Perpetual Roses which should not be overlooked. They may be called extenders rather than climbers, as they have long, whip-like shoots, and, with a little training and pruning, may be made to grow to a fair length. Mr. Darlington recommends these in preference to true rambler sorts for pillars, pointing out that they require management to keep them furnished at the base. Examples of them are Aimée Vibert, Ards Rover, Climbing Caroline Testout, Climbing F. K. Druschki, Climbing La France, and William A. Richardson. Trier and Longworth Rambler are two good late flowering varieties, and are first rate for the pergola or pillar.

It is not worth while here to go into the question of cultivation and the selection of sorts for special purposes, seeing that all this and a great deal more can be found in Mr. Darlington's excellent book on Roses, one of the "Present-Day Gardening" series.

Climbing Roses for the conservatory must not be overlooked. Is there any Rose, or any kind of flower whatever, more delicately lovely than a Maréchal Niel? It is exactly fifty years since this Rose was introduced to the public. Of unknown parentage, with a habit, foliage, and flowers that distinguish it from all other Roses, deliciously fragrant, perfect in form and colour, the Maréchal stands out by itself. It requires skill to get the plant to do its best, but, when that is accomplished, what a glorious best it is! I have seen it planted to replace Grape Vines in a large vinery, and the plants in winter produced flowers literally in thousands. That was forty years ago, when a good Maréchal Neil bud was sold for sixpence. It is one of the very best forcing Roses, but one of the worst for mildew. Still, it is no doubt first among climbing varieties for the greenhouse to-day. Next to it would come Gloire de Dijon, older even than the Maréchal. Dean Hole has said, "Were I condemned to have but one rose for the rest of my life, I should ask for a strong plant of Gloire de Dijon." It is a sturdy grower, produces flowers by the hundred, and stands glasshouse treatment well. William Allen Richardson has similar qualities. Its flowers are smaller, but in bud they are delightful, and their colour, two shades of orange or orange and cream, is pleasing. Whilst being at home in the open where Roses will grow, it is good as a greenhouse climber. It is an excellent button-hole flower.

One of the best climbing Roses where it gets what it wants, and one of the least satisfactory where the conditions are unfavourable, is the Banksia Rose. The Rev. J. H. Pemberton recently wrote in the *Garden* that "it is the most rampant of the summer-flowering Roses, and retains its mildew-proof foliage right through the winter and until the new spring growth appears; and for this reason it is the best of all Roses for covering bare walls, especially the southern front of a house, no matter how high. It will run up twelve or fifteen feet in one year, and eventually right up to the eaves, round the windows, and even over the roof. The Virginian Creeper is not in it compared with the double yellow Banksia. It never seems to grow old; twenty, thirty years hence will find it as vigorous as when it was first planted. If some cannot make it flower, the cause will probably be found in climate and treatment. As to climate, it is quite hardy, and is never injured by winter frost. But it comes into flower in May, sometimes in April. One month before it flowers the clusters of buds are formed. This is an anxious time for fruit-growers, and the weather that destroys the Peach blossom will destroy the swelling buds of the Banksia unless they are protected. The overhanging eaves of the house will generally afford the buds sufficient protection. With reference to the next point, treatment, all soils suit it, but a warm, gravelly soil, no matter how hungry and dry, is the best. No, it is not in the soil wherein lies the difficulty, but in the pruning. Unlike the *multiflora*, the strong rods made the first year will not bloom from the laterals the second year. The blooms are borne on the laterals of the laterals, and in the third year. In other words, the strong rods take three years before they bear flowers. Therefore, if we treat the Banksia as we do Crimson Rambler or Blush Rambler, for example, we shall be cutting out all the next year's flowering wood. If you have space, prune it but seldom; but if it grows beyond bounds, remove most of the strong, long-jointed rods (leaving a few for future blooming), and keep as much of the short, twiggy growth as you can, for that alone the next summer will bear flowers."

CHAPTER IX

CLEMATIS

THE history of the Clematis as a garden flower up to 1872 was well told by the late Thomas Moore, and the fullest cultural instructions, based on long experience, given by the late George Jackman in a book published by John Murray in the year named. We are there told of the increasing popularity of the Clematis as a hardy, free-flowering climber, and of the great improvement effected by breeders in the size, form, and colours of the flowers. The breeders of new varieties appear to have included continental as well as English workers, but it is doubtful if any one of them did anything like as much to make the Clematis beautiful, easy to grow, and popular, as Mr. Jackman did in his nursery at Woking, and his sons are still engaged in the task. The book referred to is probably out of print now; perhaps the proprietors could be induced to bring out a new edition of it, for beyond the fact that more crosses have been made and a number of species added to those grown forty years ago, there isn't much to be said that has not already been well said by Messrs. Moore and Jackman in their book, *The Clematis.*

The first hybrid Clematis recorded was raised in 1835 in Henderson's Pine-apple Nursery, St. John's Wood.

This was followed by many seedlings of Belgian origin. M. Lemoine, Nancy; Messrs. Simon-Louis, Metz; M. Carré, Troyes; M. Briolay-Goiffon, M. Dauvesse, Orleans; and Herr Rinz, Frankfort, were other pioneer breeders of Clematis. Messrs. Cripps & Son, Tunbridge Wells, were among the foremost breeders and growers of them in England, and down to quite recently their nursery was famous for its collection of varieties. Mr. Charles Noble, Sunningdale, also raised many, whilst the late Mr. Anderson-Henry, Edinburgh, was easily first among amateur raisers of new hybrids.

According to Moore and Jackman the species from which all the earlier hybrids and seedlings were derived were *C. patens*, *C. lanuginosa*, *C. Fortunei*, now called *C. florida*, and *C. Standishii*, and as Standishii is now reckoned a variety of *C. patens*, we have three species only, all Japanese, as the progenitors of the army of named sorts (180 are listed in Moore and Jackman's book) raised and grown in gardens up to the end of the nineteenth century.

To these have to be added the crosses of recent origin, those between *C. coccinea* and various garden sorts being perhaps the most distinct. They have smaller, fleshier flowers than the *patens-lanuginosa* type, and although less showy, perhaps, they possess both grace and beauty. Still more recent are the crosses between *C. montana* and the big-flowered garden sorts; this section is also a decided gain.

The possibilities of Clematis now are endless, a number of distinct species having been introduced, mainly from China, during the last ten years or so, and as the genus appears to respond readily to the attentions of the

PLATE VI

CLEMATIS NELLY MOSER

hybridiser, he can if he wishes ring all sorts of changes with them. The best of the new introductions are:

C. montana rubens: Flowers claret-coloured, produced in May.

C. tangutica: Yellow-flowered. Often in bloom in November.

C. Meyeniana: Flowers white, in large, loose panicles. A robust evergreen.

C. Armandii (see Plate VII): A tall climber, evergreen, with large bold cymes of white, Anemone-like flowers.

C. Dennisæ (*Sanderi*): The Australian form of *C. indivisa*, evergreen, the long shoots crowded with axillary panicles of white star-like flowers, the red and yellow stamens forming a conspicuous brush-like cluster in the centre of each star.

C. Wilsonii: A long-stalked, large, white-flowered variety of the polymorphic *C. montana*, flowering in late autumn.

C. Sieboldii (see Plate IX): A new Clematis with neatly formed white perianth of six segments, showing off finely a central mass of purple, linear, modified, barren stamens. Flowers 3½ inches' diameter.

The cultural requirements of Clematis may be called quite ordinary. They prefer a loamy soil, light rather than heavy, and they like lime or chalk mixed with it in the proportion of a spadeful to a barrowload. They also enjoy an annual mulch with rotten farmyard manure, which should be applied in winter. The shoots are self-supporting, but they require a little arranging at the start. Where there is plenty of room the less pruning they get the better; all that is needed being a kind of combing out to get rid of brash and prevent overcrowding. This should be done in early spring before new growth starts. In some positions, however, a decided pruning may be necessary, and some varieties in some positions require to be annually close pruned; this should be done in spring. The *Jackmanii* race is the hardiest and most useful of all because of its good nature and free summer and autumn flowering habit. The many forms of it may be used in various ways, either on pergolas, arches, summer-houses, verandahs, pillars, house fronts, old trees, or as trailers over rock-work. Hop-pole treatment is not unsuitable for them; they may also supplant Ivy as drapery for old walls, and ruins.

The general method of propagation for Clematises is by grafting, done in warmth in early spring or even winter. The stock used is the fleshy root of *C. Vitalba*, and the scion a young shoot, or portion of one, prepared for the purpose by forcing into early growth the plant of which stock is required. With proper appliances and just that skill in cutting and fitting which is got by experience, it is easy to raise any number of plants of a given variety, or, at any rate, as many as there are scions available, for the expert grafter does not anticipate a single failure.

But grafting is not really necessary; one might go further and say it is not the best way to propagate Clematises. On this point I will quote here what Professor Balfour stated in his *Problems of Propagation*: "The common belief is that Clematises are difficult to strike, and propagation by grafting is frequently adopted. They are really not difficult to strike from cuttings, if the cutting be made through an internode. Internodal cuttings may be struck within a fortnight. It is otherwise if nodal cuttings are used. These callus well—profusely indeed—but refuse to form roots either from the callus or from the stem above it. Doubtless this has given rise to the widely spread belief that it is difficult to strike cuttings of Clematis. An internodal cutting is a portion of a shoot, the base of which, instead of being just below the joint or node, is some dis-

PLATE VII. CLEMATIS ARMANDII

tance lower down, an inch or so below the node. There appear to be a number of plants for which the internodal cutting is preferable to the other. Why there should be this difference has not been explained." The node is the point where the leaf axils with their buds occur, and the internode the stem intervening between two nodes.

As to the cultivation of Clematis and the up-to-date sorts worth growing, Messrs. Jackman & Son, Woking, who specialise in these plants, say the best time to plant is October and November, or in the spring. They recommend for each plant the digging of a hole 2 feet deep and square, and loosening the bottom before putting in prepared soil. The hole should first be partly filled in, the plant being then carefully taken out of the pot and the crocks removed, setting the ball in the middle and filling up with more soil, pressing it firmly, so that when finished the ball of roots shall be from 1½ to 2 inches below the surface of the ground; finally, the soil should be booted firm round the plant. Being rampant growers, Clematis prefer a moist soil, though thorough drainage is indispensable to good healthy development; and the vigour of the plant must be kept up by annual manurings with horse or cow manure. On dry, hot soils cow manure would probably be preferable, whilst on heavy soils a thorough dressing of good leaf-mould would be beneficial. Mulching with half-rotten dung is another mode of manuring; the operation should be performed annually on the approach of winter, its effect being to increase the strength of the plant and the size of the flowers.

Pruning is one of the important points of good management. The pruning of the varieties belonging to the *Calycinæ*, *Anemonifloræ*, *Azuræ*, *Floridæ*, and *Lanuginosæ* types should take place in the months of February or March, and consist in removing the weak, straggling, or overcrowded branches. Some sorts flower from the old or ripened wood ; therefore, to secure blossoms, the strong, one-year-old wood should be trained in, as far as it has become thoroughly ripened, beyond which it may be cut away, the retained parts being so disposed as to fill up vacant spaces. The varieties of the *Viticellæ* and *Jackmanii* types being summer and autumn bloomers, flowering on the young or summer shoots, the aim in pruning should be to favour the development of vigorous young shoots, by cutting back the summer growth each season, say in November. The ground should then be mulched, as advised above. The varieties of the *Viornæ* section should have the shoots cut off to where they have died down.

The following list is from Messrs. Jackman's catalogue:

CALYCINÆ

Evergreen climbing winter bloomers, with small flowers borne in January and February on the old or ripened wood.

C. calycina (*balearica*)*:* Creamy-white, dotted on inside with purple spots.

C. cirrhosa: White, evergreen, winter-flowering.

ANEMONIFLORÆ

Spring bloomers. The medium-sized flowers are borne in axillary clusters on the old and ripened wood in May.

C. montana: White, Wood Anemone-like.

C. montana grandiflora: White.

C. montana rubens: Claret-red, autumn flowering.

PLATE VIII. CLEMATIS HENRYI

AZURÆ

Large-flowered spring bloomers, flowering from the old or ripened wood in May and June.

Fair Rosamond: Bluish-white, with an indistinct, wine-red bar.
Lady Londesborough: Silver-grey, paler bar.
Miss Bateman: White, chocolate-red anthers.
Miss Crawshay: Solferino-pink.
Mrs. George Jackman: Satiny-white with creamy bar.
Sir Garnet Wolseley: Bluish ground with bar of plum-red.
Stella: Light violet with bar of deep red.
The Queen: Delicate lavender.

FLORIDÆ

Large-flowered summer bloomers, flowering from the old or ripened wood. The following all bear double flowers:

Belle of Woking: Silvery-grey. June.
Countess of Lovelace: Bluish-lilac, rosette-shaped. June, July.
Duchess of Edinburgh: The best of the double whites, deliciously scented. June, July.
Lucie Lemoine: White, rosette-shaped, pale yellow anthers. June, July.

LANUGINOSÆ

Large-flowered summer and autumn bloomers, flowering successionally on short, lateral summer shoots from July to October.

Alba Magna: Pure white, remarkably broad sepals.
Beauty of Worcester: Bluish-violet, with prominent white stamens, produces single and double blooms.
Bella Nantoise: Delicate lavender.
Blue Gem: Pale cerulean-blue.
Fairy Queen: Pale flesh, with pink bar.
Gloire de St. Julien: White, with yellow stamens, very large.

Grand Duchess: Bluish-white.

Henryi (see Plate VIII): Large, finely formed, creamy-white.

Imperatrice Eugenie: Large pure white.

Jeanne D'Arc: Greyish-white.

King Edward VII: Violet-purple with bars of crimson.

Lady Caroline Neville: French-white, mauve bars.

La France: Deep violet-purple.

Lanuginosa candida: Greyish-white.

Lawsoniana: Rosy-purple with darker veins.

Lord Neville: Dark plum colour.

Madame Van Houtte: White, suffused with mauve.

Marcel Moser: Mauve-violet with red bar.

Marie Boisselot: Pure white.

Mrs. Hope: Satiny-mauve, bar darker.

Nelly Moser (see Plate VI): Light mauve with bright red bar, large.

Otto Froebel: Greyish-white, very large.

Princess of Wales: Deep bluish-mauve with a satiny surface.

Purpurea elegans: Deep violet-purple.

Queen Alexandra: Pale lavender with lilac-purple base, silvery-white down the centre.

Robert Hanbury: Bluish-lilac edged with red.

Sensation: Rich satiny-mauve.

William Kennett: Deep lavender.

VITICELLÆ

Large-flowered summer and autumn bloomers, flowering continuously in profuse masses on summer shoots.

Ascotensis: Azure-blue, large.

Kermesina: Bright red.

Madame Grange: Crimson-violet with red bar.

Ville de Lyon: Carmine-red, a deeper shade round the edges.

Viticella alba: Greyish-white.

" " *luxurians:* White, very free.

PLATE IX. CLEMATIS SIEBOLDII

JACKMANII

Mostly large-flowered, flowering successionally in profuse, continuous masses on summer shoots from July to October.

Alexandra: Pale reddish-violet.
Comtesse de Bouchaud: Satiny-rose.
Gipsy Queen: Dark velvety-purple.
Guiding Star: Purplish, shaded crimson.
Jackmanii: Violet-purple, very floriferous.
" *alba:* White.
" *rubra:* A red-purple variety of the same habit and as floriferous as its parent.
" *superba:* Dark violet-purple.
Madame Edouard Andre: Bright velvety-red, free.
Magnifica: Purple with red bars.
Mrs. Cholmondeley: Light blue.
Prince of Wales: Deep pucy-purple.
Rubella: Rich claret-purple.
Snow White Jackmanni: Free-flowering white.
Star of India: Reddish-plum with red bars.
The President: Deep violet, reddish towards the centre.
Thomas Moore: Rich purple-violet.
Tunbridgensis: Bluish-mauve.
Velutina purpurea: Blackish-mulberry.

PANICULATÆ

Small-flowered, blooming profusely on summer shoots from July to October.

Buchaniana: Pale yellow, sweet-scented.
Flammula: White, sweet-scented.
" *rosea purpurea:* Rosy-purple, sweet-scented.
Graveolens: Yellow.
Paniculata: White.
Vitalba: White, "Traveller's Joy."

VIORNÆ

Climbing, sub-shrubby, flowering successionally on summer shoots from July to September.

Coccinea: Scarlet.
Crispa: Pinkish-white, sweet-scented.

CHAPTER X

IVIES

THESE exceedingly useful plants have already been praised in this volume. Forty years ago, before gardening books were anything like so plentiful as now, they formed the subject of a charming monograph by Shirley Hibberd. If there is one leaf thoroughly well known to every British man, woman, and child, it must be the leaf of the Ivy, for it thrives in the most unpromising corners of the smokiest towns, and there are also abundant opportunities for seeing it growing wild in the country. It is one of the most universally popular of all plants, a circumstance which is no doubt somewhat assisted by the meaning attached to Ivy in the so-called language of flowers: it stands for friendship, and has the mottoes, "I cling to thee," and "I die where I am attached." Ivy is the badge of the Clan Gordon.

Seeing that Ivy was associated with both Christian and Pagan festivals, it is not remarkable that it should have been adopted as a tavern sign, being, no doubt, derived from the very ancient sign of "The Bush," which was introduced to this country by the Romans, and which is the explanation of the proverb, "Good wine needs no bush."

PLATE X. SOLANUM JASMINOIDES GROWING OVER PATHWAY

Although Ivy is so generally beloved it has been repeatedly assailed by a few people on two grounds. Regarding the first, that its presence on trees is injurious to them, this cannot be gainsaid. It has a strangling effect and checks the circulation of sap. In course of time Ivy will kill the strongest tree. But the idea that the plant is a parasite capable of obtaining nourishment from a living host is erroneous.

The second objection to Ivy concerns its presence on buildings. Those keenly alive to architectural beauties assert that a cloak of vulgar Ivy in many cases conceals the builder's greatest triumphs; and many people believe that it renders buildings damp. As regards covering what is beautiful it is obvious that some discrimination should be exercised, but it cannot be denied that very often, in masking the ugly, Ivy is a public benefactor. A wall originally damp becomes drier when Ivy-clothed, for the leaves shoot off the rain, and the stem-roots suck the moisture from the fabric to feed the plant.

Few plants are as variable as *Hedera Helix.* But it is only within the last half century that much advantage has been taken of this peculiarity. As the result of Ivy hunting in the woods, purchases from gardens, and cross-breeding, Mr. Hibberd obtained more than two hundred varieties, many of them with the most diverse characteristics. Fifty of the best were named and put into commerce, and others have since been added. The Kew *Hand-list of Trees and Shrubs* contains ninety-three varieties, all represented in the cultivated collection, and the best nurserymen offer ample selections.

One of the museums at Kew forms an object-lesson in being charmingly clothed with a wealth of the best and most distinct varieties. The main collection of Ivies at the National Garden will be found growing over the upturned butts of trees. At Kew, also, it can be seen to what great advantage Ivy may be used to cover the bare, shaded ground beneath trees, while prominent among the various ways in which this ubiquitous, general utility plant is made effective use of are its being made to grow over posts about eight feet high, which stand at intervals in beds occupied by low-growing shrubs, and to cover balustrades and what would otherwise be an unsightly barrier of hanging chains. The grafted, so-called tree Ivies have their distinct uses.

It may be repeated that Ivy is unequalled for covering bare places under trees. Ivy on walls is much improved in appearance by being clipped once a year. It is not so harmful to buildings as some people suppose, but, although picturesque, a covering of Ivy is very bad for trees. *Algeriensis variegata*, *atropurpurea*, *aurea elegantissima*, *digitata*, *flavescens*, *Maderiensis variegata*, *marginata media*, *palmata aurea*, *rhombea*, and *triloba* are some of the best of the climbing varieties. Cuttings root very easily out of doors.

CHAPTER XI

VINES

THE term vine belongs properly to *Vitis vinifera*, the Grape Vine, the wine-bearer, but in the United States it has come to be used for any trailing, climbing, or running stem. The same loose application of terms is to be observed in the use of Rose, Lily, and Apple. The Americans are given

Plate XI. CLIANTHUS PUNICEUS AND OTHER CLIMBING PLANTS IN THE GREENHOUSE, KEW

to this sort of thing; they call Ampelopsis Boston Ivy, *Cobœa scandens* is their Cup and Saucer Vine, and *Cissus discolor* they have named the Climbing Begonia, as if there were not true Begonias that are climbers! In this country, when we speak of Vines we mean Grape Vines, although there is a tendency to describe as Vines all the species of Vitis, which is as illogical as it would be to call all Pyruses pears, or all Prunuses plums.

The Vine is a king among climbing plants. Where it grows wild it clings to tall trees, covering them with a luxuriant canopy of handsome foliage and fruiting abundantly. Man has tamed it and made it contribute both food and drink. How he has succeeded, everybody knows. Here we are to consider the Vine only as an ornamental climber, in which aspect it is still a king. Gardeners appear to overlook its claims, except as a producer of grapes. If only they would plant it where it could have full liberty of growth, against buildings, arches, arbours, pergolas, verandahs, trees, or to run along the top of an old wall, the charm of its stems and leaves would perhaps enlighten them. In autumn the colours of the leaves equal those of any oak, thorn, or maple, whilst at all times their form is delightful, to the artistic eye at any rate.

There is a variety, called *purpurea,* which has leaves of port-wine colour, especially in autumn, and another, called *laciniosa,* with elegantly slashed leaves. But one need not trouble about varieties, except perhaps for exposed positions, where Royal Muscadine, or Chasselas Vibert, or Grove End Sweetwater would most likely do best, and with good fortune these would probably bear bunches of palatable fruit. Indeed, the varieties of the Grape Vine are very numerous. It is said that the French Government once made a collection of them, and they got together in a nursery at Luxembourg 1400 varieties, and this did not exhaust the number!

As Barron says, the Vine will grow in any good garden soil, provided it is well drained, and the position is light and airy. It is perfectly hardy so far as growth is concerned, our climate being deficient only where the production of good fruit every year is the object; then glass-house protection is needed.

There are other species of Vitis which have the habit of growth and the large, handsome foliage of *V. vinifera;* moreover, they are as hardy and as easy to manage as that plant is. Altogether some thirty species are of this character, every one good growers and effective in the garden. Some are North Americans; for example, *V. Labrusca*, the Fox Grape, *V. vulpina*, which, from its name, should be the Wolf Grape, *V. cordifolia*, *V. æstivalis* and *V. californica*, the last named a first-class plant in this country. Of Asiatic species the best, in addition to the Grape Vine, are *V. Thunbergii*, *V. Romanetii*, *V. Davidii* (Spinovitis), and *V. Coignetiæ*. The Hop-leaved *V. heterophylla* is not a strong grower, but it has elegant foliage, and there is a variety of it with variegated leaves. The great delight of the Hop-leaved Vine is its turquoise-blue berries, shining like porcelain, really more like a work of art than the unaided effort of a climber on the wall. They are rather small and in clusters. The plant only thrives in a sunny, sheltered position.

The newer species from China have not yet fully shown what they can do here, though so far they promise very well. Messrs. Veitch, with the assistance of Wilson, imported quite a number of them, which they have exhibited

PLATE XII. VITIS ARMATA VEITCHII

periodically at flower shows. The best appear to be *V. megaphylla,* with large bipinnate leaves, quite unlike the ordinary run of Vines; *V. Thomsonii,* which has digitate leaves of a purple colour; and *V. armata,* with prickly stems. Other named Chinese species of Veitchian introduction are *V. Delavayi, V. flexuosa, V. obtecta, V. serjanæfolia* and *V. armata Veitchii* (see Plate XII).

We owe to China a better knowledge of *V. Thunbergii,* formerly confused with the American *V. Labrusca.* Its foliage at the close of summer assumes rich colours—crimson, green, and yellow; and in the warmer parts of the British Islands it is quite happy in the open air. In the garden of Canon Ellacombe, Bitton, for example, it is a striking object. At the same time it is not equal to *V. Coignetiæ,* also Chinese, which in the nursery of Mr. A. Waterer, Woking, is magnificent in autumn, when the leaves are at their best. One has only to see it to realise the value of the big-leaved species of Vitis as garden plants.

CHAPTER XII

ORNAMENTAL GOURDS

"THERE be divers gourds, some wild, others tame, for the garden, some bearing fruit like unto a bottle; others longer and bigger at the end, keeping no certain fashion." Thus Gerard, in his *Herbal,* modestly describes the family of the Melon, Cucumber, Pumpkin, Loofah, Colocynth, Squash, Calabash, and Choco. Economically considered, the Gourd family is of great value to man as supplying food, medicine, ornament, musical instruments, and domestic utensils.

Here we need only consider those members of it which have a value as decorative garden plants.

Tropical Gourds are always well represented in one of the stoves at Kew. They are trained to wires under the roof, where they get plenty of sunshine; and being planted in a border of rich soil, pretty much as Cucumbers and Melons are, they grow and fruit freely. Formerly they were grown in the Palm House, their stems being trained to upright rods reaching from floor to roof. Most of the species cultivated are raised annually from seeds sown in February, the young plants being grown in pots until they are half a yard or so high and are strong enough to be planted in the border. This is about 18 inches wide and deep, and is formed of turf and good loam and manure on a slate shelf about a yard above the floor. It will be seen from these particulars that the treatment is essentially that practised by the market grower for Cucumbers. That it is successful will be admitted by anyone who has seen the plants in fruit at Kew in autumn. They include species of the following genera: Benincasa, Citrullus, Cucumis, Cucurbita, Gurania, Lagenaria, Luffa, Momordica, Sechium, Telfairia, and Trichosanthes.

Sixty years ago Sir William Hooker wrote: "One of the tropical stoves at Kew has been rendered attractive for some years past by the introduction of various cucurbitaceous plants trained against the roof. It is a family of plants that has been too much neglected, for they present no small degree of beauty in their flowers, and their fruits are remarkable in their size, or form, or colour, and often their utility." These words are just as true to-day as they were sixty years ago. How many gardeners who have to furnish large conservatories ever think of including cucurbitaceous plants among the climbers? Yet there are few more effective objects than a Snake Gourd when in fruit, or a Jove's Club, or a Bottle Gourd, or a Hedgehog Gourd. When *Momordica mixta* first fruited in the Water Lily House some twenty years ago it created quite a sensation. The male plant (some of the species are diœcious) had been grown at Kew many years before a female was obtained. Both sexes bear large, handsome, star-shaped flowers, creamy-white with an eye-like blotch of purple; but the glory of this Gourd is its fruit, which is larger than an ostrich egg, and, when ripe, a glowing crimson. Another pretty species of the same genus is *M. involucrata,* which has thin stems, Ampelopsis-like leaves, bell-shaped flowers, and ovate fruits 2 inches long, coloured scarlet. *M. Charantia* and *M. muricata* have equally attractive fruit, and when they split open they reveal rows of large seeds of purple colour. Surely the Snake Gourds (Trichosanthes), with their white, deep-fringed flowers, are worth a place among pretty flowered plants; moreover, when their long, writhing, brightly coloured fruits are ripe, they are as fantastic as they are decorative.

The great variety of form in the fruits of the Gourd family is indicated by their popular names, such as Apple, Orange, Pear, Gooseberry, Bottle, Custard, Club, Snake, Turban, &c. Nathaniel Hawthorne has said that if ever Providence made him wealthy, he would have a service of plate or porcelain wrought in the shape of Gourds of his own growing.

A considerable number of Gourds may be cultivated out of doors in this country. Being all sun lovers, they must be allowed all the direct sunlight possible. This can be best managed by training them on rough poles or on arches, arbours, or pergolas. A pergola devoted entirely to Gourds could easily be made a striking feature in summer. The plants require to be grown on in warmth, raising them from seeds sown in spring, and as they will not stand frost, they must not be set outside before the first week in June. Lateral shoots must be stopped and the flowers fertilised to ensure a set of fruits. The soil for them should be light and rich, say a mixture of loam, three parts, and well rotted stable manure, one part. They must be kept fairly moist at the root, watering in dry weather being necessary. A mulch with light manure is helpful to growth and fruitfulness, and it does most good if applied about mid-August. In dry, hot weather the plants are all the better for a sousing overhead with water in the evening.

There is a very good list of showy fruited Gourds, with figures of many of them, in Robinson's *Vegetable Garden*, an English edition of *Les Plantes Potagères*, by Messrs. Vilmorin-Andrieux & Co., which, by the way, is a most comprehensive and trustworthy work on garden vegetables of all kinds. There they are described under the headings of Cucumbers, Gourds, Pumpkins, Melons, and Fancy Gourds. The seeds are cheap, and whilst it has to be remembered that the plants of this family intercross readily, thus rendering purity of race somewhat precarious, the seeds supplied by respectable dealers are fairly true to name.

PLATE XIII

IPOMŒA RUBRO-CŒRULEA

F. Ernest Waltham

CHAPTER XIII

AROIDS

A NUMBER of species of tropical Aroids are climbers. They form long, rope-like stems which attach themselves to the trunks of trees by means of aerial roots after the manner of Ivy. Some of them are like Ivy, too, in being dimorphic, the strictly climbing stems having comparatively small leaves and clinging quite close to their support, as Ivy does, whilst the later, mature stage of the plant is characterised by large leaves and a less clinging habit. Some of the Philodendrons develop stems a hundred yards long; they climb to the tops of the highest trees and then, liana-like, extend from tree to tree, their long, string-like, aerial roots often reaching the ground, where they take firm root, and become quite taut. In large tropical houses these climbing Aroids may be turned to excellent account for covering walls or clothing pillars with striking vegetation. Their value for these purposes is displayed in the Aroid House (No. 1) and the Palm House at Kew. Here the genera Anthurium, Philodendron, Epipremnum, Monstera, Rhaphidophora, Scindapsus, and Pothos are represented by many species, and some of them are as remarkable for their large, handsome, often fragrant flowers as for their magnificent foliage.

These Aroids all enjoy a warm, moist atmosphere and plenty of moisture in the soil, and they are as easy to propagate from stem cuttings as Ivy is. Once started at the foot of a wall, pillar, or Palm trunk they do all the rest themselves, clinging, climbing, and developing their leaves, and later producing their flowers annually with no assistance from the gardener except in summer a daily drenching with water, which they like, and in most cases, an annual pruning to keep them within bounds. A selection of species of the different genera mentioned should include the following: *Anthurium Andreanum*, *Epipremnum mirabile*, *E. giganteum*, *Monstera deliciosa*, *M. dilacerata*, *M. obliqua*, *M. tenuis* (*Marcgravia paradoxa*), *Philodendron Andreanum*, *P. Corsianum*, *P. Carderi*, *P. crinitum*, *P. erubescens*, *P. gloriosum*, *P. laciniosum*, *P. nobile*, *P. Mamei*, *P. ornatum*, *P. Selloum*, *P. verrucosum*, *Pothos argenteus*, *P. celatocaulis*, *P. scandens*, *Rhaphidophora decursiva*, *R. lancifolia*, *R. pertusa*, *Scindapsus hederaceus*, *S. perakensis*, *S. pictus*, *S. pteropodus*.

One of the plants included in this list deserves more than mere mention, and that is *Monstera deliciosa*. It has stout clinging stems as thick as a man's wrist, and its roots encircle the trunk of a tree like strong twine. Its leaves are nearly a yard wide, heart-shaped, the margins sometimes deeply slashed (laciniated), the blade pierced with large perforations between the principal veins. This character alone distinguishes the plant from all others. From the axils of the stout, sheathing leaf-stalks enormous arm-like flowers are developed; they consist of a boat-shaped, fleshy, yellow spathe, inside which is a thick cylindrical spadix, composed of a large number of fleshy white pistils, arranged spirally, with the short, thick anthers between. This spadix enlarges and finally becomes an elongated cone, about a pound in weight, green, not unlike a pine-apple, and when ripe it is as juicy, fragrant, and delicious in flavour as any pine-apple. The "pips" separate readily. Writing about this tropical Aroid fifty years ago Dr. Lindley said: "Viewed as a fruit-bearing plant its interest is exceptional; for although it is some years growing to a flowering age and the fruit takes twelve months to ripen, yet as supplying a novel article of dessert of the richest and most *recherché* character, it might be usefully cultivated for its produce in those establishments where a variety of fruits is prized and where space can be afforded." The plants at Kew fruit annually, and when at their best their fragrance permeates the whole house.

Another remarkable species of Monstera, introduced from Nicaragua in 1870, was for many years cultivated under the name of *Marcgravia paradoxa*. In its juvenile or clinging form this plant has leaves of the size and shape of average oyster shells, which, together with the stem, are pressed flat against a tree trunk, up which it climbs for 12 or 15 feet, when it changes in habit and the leaves become nearly a yard long and wide, deeply pinnate as in some big Polypodium, and no more like the juvenile leaves than a penny is like a peacock's feather. Another plant, known in some gardens as *Pothos aurea*, and having when young short-stalked, roundish, ovate leaves 6 inches long and coloured green and yellow, grew up at Kew into a big, pinnate-leaved Rhaphidophora.

Marcgravia proper is a genus which may be briefly described here. The species are epiphytic climbers, dimorphic, as the Ivy is, the juvenile leaves being small and pressed flat against the host plant, whilst those on mature shoots are thick and fleshy, and these shoots do not attempt to cling. The flowers are known to be handsome, but although I have known several species in cultivation, for many years not one has ever been induced to flower. The common species is *M. umbellata*, a native of Tropical America. It is a good plant to serve the purpose of Ivy under tropical conditions.

CHAPTER XIV

CLIMBING ORCHIDS

It is remarkable that in an order of such magnitude as Orchidaceæ, with a very wide distribution and so rich in species of epiphytic habit, there are very few species that are climbers. Orchids have small, light seeds, which are easily carried considerable distances by the wind and other agencies, and they are thus naturally placed in suitable positions for growth. Their clinging roots enable them to fasten themselves firmly to the branches of trees, and as they can obtain all the nourishment they require from the humus collected in the fissures of the bark, or the dead cortical layer of the bark itself and that provided by the atmosphere, few have any occasion to climb. They are not quite so dependent as, say, the Mistletoe, but they have very little chance of prospering unless they can fasten on to the backs of other stronger plants. A number of them so develop fairly long stems, and so far as they go they behave like climbers; but their extended growth is in search of fresh root-hold and not a struggle for a place in the sun. There are, however, several genera which have a claim to a place in a treatise on climbing plants, namely, Renanthera, Vanda, and Vanilla.

RENANTHERA

This Eastern genus of about half-a-dozen species, all with an elongated stem, is best known in gardens by *R. coccinea,* which has stems sometimes 20 feet long. It clings by means of stem roots, and when it is happy it produces a magnificent panicle of butterfly-like scarlet flowers. It can only be grown successfully in a large house. I have seen it in great glory in the large conservatory at Chatsworth, where it had grown to the top of a birch-tree trunk about 20 feet high, which was well furnished with the stems and roots of the Orchid. It is grown in the same way in the Mexican House at Kew, where it flowers now and then. *R. coccinea* grows in woods in Cochin China. It is cultivated in the gardens of China for its gorgeous flowers, of course. One of the oldest plants in the famous collection of Orchids formed by the late Sir Trevor Lawrence was a specimen of *R. coccinea,* which in 1911 had been in his possession thirty-three years, and was said to have been brought to this country from China as long ago as 1815.

VANDA

This large and varied genus contains two species which may be called climbers, namely, *V. teres* and *V. Hookeriana.* The former is wild in the woods of Lower Bengal and other parts of India, where its stems grow to a length of many feet and attach themselves to trees by means of their stem roots. In this country we do not allow the stems to grow to any length—a yard at the most being considered long enough; and as the plant will stand beheading like any Cactus, and is supposed to flower all the better for it, there does not appear to be any good reason for letting it grow longer. However, it is undoubtedly a climbing Orchid, and one would like to see it grown as such. There is no saying what stems 20 feet or so long would produce in the way of flowers.

V. Hookeriana, a native of Malaya, has the habit and general characters of *V. teres;* but the leaves are shorter, the scape is longer, and the flowers are about half the size of that species. The colour of *V. teres* is white or rose, the lip being yellow or purple; that of *V. Hookeriana* is a delicate yellow and pink, with a purple and white lip. There are not many old plants of *V. Hookeriana* in cultivation in British collections, for it is rather a difficult plant to keep in health. On the other hand, few Orchids are easier than *V. teres*. Both species enjoy sunshine and plenty of water in the growing season.

VANILLA

Vanilla is a genus of climbers. About fifty species have been described, but only one of them has any claim to consideration as a garden plant, and that is *Vanilla planifolia*, which yields the Vanilla of commerce. A native of Mexico, it is now widely cultivated in tropical countries. "From historical accounts we know that Vanilla was used by the Aztecs of Mexico as an ingredient in the manufacture of chocolate prior to the discovery of America by the Spaniards, who adopted its use; and Morren states that it was brought to Europe as a perfume about the year 1510, at the same time as indigo, cochineal, and cacao, and ten years before the arrival of tobacco" (*Kew Bulletin*).

The plant is said to have been in cultivation in this country in 1807, when, according to Andrews, it flowered in the garden of the Right Hon. Charles Greville at Paddington. Professor Charles Morren, Liége, was the first to produce fruit of it in quantity. He obtained fifty-four flowers on one plant, which he fertilised artificially, and every one developed a pod. Morren suggested that Vanilla might be made to pay as a cultivated crop in this country if the plants were properly grown and the flowers artificially fertilised. In recent times Vanilla pods have been produced in quantity by plants grown at Syon, Kew, and elsewhere. The plant is worth growing in any stove with a view to its fruiting, the odour of the "beans" when they are ripe being particularly agreeable. The rope-like stems grow to a length of 20 feet or more. They have white aerial roots, and oblong fleshy leaves about 8 inches long. The flowers are produced in short racemes from the leaf axils, and are Cattleya-like; and 4 inches across, cream yellow, with a few lines of orange on the lip. The beans are about 8 inches long. The plant requires moist tropical conditions. It will cling to a wall by means of its roots, or it can be trained on wires under a roof. There is a prettily variegated form of it in cultivation.

CHAPTER XV

ALPHABETICAL LIST OF GENERA

In the following chapter the genera are taken in alphabetical order. The most useful species are selected for remark in each case in the hope that these will be more useful to amateurs than printing exhaustive lists. The cultural advice is based on knowledge obtained and long experience.

ABELIA

The species of Abelia are showy shrubs of the Honeysuckle order, which in most parts of the country require the protection of walls. Only two species are much grown. *A. chinensis* (*rupestris*), Rock Abelia, the hardiest, is of close habit, and its white, pink-tinted, fragrant flowers appear in late summer. *A. floribunda*, Mexican Abelia, bears drooping clusters of long-lasting, rosy-purple flowers, and is worthy of cultivation under glass. Both are evergreen. Abelias prefer light soil, and are propagated by cuttings in summer, or by layers in spring. Among the rarer species, *A. triflora* and *A. spathulata* deserve mention.

ABUTILON

The taller-growing species and garden varieties of Abutilon, of which there are a large number, some remarkable for floral beauty and others for ornamental foliage, are well adapted for growing as greenhouse roof or pillar plants. *A. Darwinii*, bright orange flowers with darker veinings, *A. megapotamicum*, red and yellow flowers, and *A. venosum*, very large orange flowers with red veins, with their forms and hybrids, rank high among greenhouse climbers, besides being useful for outdoor summer effect. They succeed best planted out in loam and peat. Cuttings of the young wood strike freely in early spring or in September. When growing they should be fed liberally, but require to be kept almost dry from late autumn until the end of winter.

ACACIA

Some of the cultivated species of this large genus of Leguminosæ make long, straight shoots, and are well adapted for training on greenhouse rafters or pillars, where they are very effective when in flower from Christmas onwards. They are *A. Baileyana*, *A. leprosa*, *A. retinodes*,

PLATE XIV. YELLOW ABUTILON

and *A. Riceana.* These will flourish in a temperature little above freezing point in winter. They should be pruned after flowering, and when grown in pots they are all the better for spending the summer in the open air. Propagation is effected by seeds, or cuttings of half-ripened wood with a heel. A few of the species are successful as outdoor plants in exceptionally mild districts.

ACONITUM

One of the Monk's Hoods, *Aconitum uncinatum*, a North American hardy perennial, attains as much as 8 feet in height, with branched stems and large lilac-coloured flowers in loose racemes. It succeeds well in partial shade, and is easily propagated by root division, or from seeds sown as soon as ripe in a cold frame.

ACTINIDIA

Hardy and ornamental deciduous summer-flowering shrubs, related to Camellia, and mostly natives of China and Japan. They have axillary corymbs of waxy white or yellow flowers. They should be planted in rich soil. *A. Kolomikta,* which should have the shelter of a wall, has its leaves beautifully tinted in autumn. *A. chinensis,* of strong climbing habit, has edible fruits with the flavour of ripe gooseberries. *A. polygama* has fragrant flowers, and *A. volubilis* (twining) is very free in growth. Increased by seeds, layers, or cuttings taken in autumn.

AKEBIA

A. lobata and *A. quinata* are pretty, strong-growing shrubs from China and Japan, which are hardy in most places. Their purple flowers (male and female), borne in drooping racemes, are succeeded by curious sausage-like fruits, violet in colour when ripe. They make good trellis plants, or may be allowed to ramble over other shrubs. Sandy loam with peat suits them best, and they can be increased by cuttings taken in summer, or by division.

ALLAMANDA (see Plate XV)

Allamandas form scandent, deciduous shrubs; their long, free-growing stems are clothed with whorls of large laurel-like leaves which enable the plants to climb trees. Their fragrant flowers, usually very large and bell-shaped with wide-spreading lobes, are borne in axillary racemes, and in all the species except *A. violacea* they are yellow. *A cathartica*, *A. grandiflora*, *A. nobilis*, *A. Schottii*, with its vars. *Hendersonii* and *magnifica*, and *A. violacea*, are well-known garden plants. They are all robust growers except *A. grandiflora*, which is happiest when grafted on *A. Schottii*. They may be trained against pillars or rafters in tropical houses, or by pruning they may be grown as shrubs supported by a stake. In winter they require to be kept dry at the root, and in March the shoots should be cut back to short spurs. The prunings may be used as cuttings, for they strike root freely.

AMPELOPSIS

Fast-growing and ornamental hardy deciduous shrubs, of very easy cultivation in any soil or situation, and brilliantly coloured in autumn. Ampelopsis is nearly allied to Vitis, and is incorporated therein by some

PLATE XV

ALLAMANDA SCHOTTII HENDERSONII

botanists, as well as having been endowed with other names. The best known are: *A. quinquefolia* (*hederacea*), Virginian Creeper, of which there is a superior variety called *muralis* or *Englemannii*, more capable of clinging to a bare wall without other support: *Veitchii* (syn. *A. tricuspidata*, *Vitis inconstans*, &c.), a native of Japan, with short branched tendrils provided with suckers, capable of holding fast to any surface; not quite so finely coloured in autumn as *A. quinquefolia*, but to be preferred to it; and *A. bipinnata*, North America, a beautiful plant, less rapid in growth than the preceding. Propagation is effected by cuttings, either inserted outdoors under a hand light in September, or in moderate heat in the spring.

ARAUJIA (Physianthus)

Free growing climbers with hairy, ovate leaves, and white or pink Stephanotis-like flowers; natives of tropical and sub-tropical America. The best species are *A. grandiflora* and *A. sericifera* (*albens*) (see Plate XVI), both white flowered, and they can be grown either in the stove or the greenhouse. They require a compost of sandy loam and peat, with good drainage. Propagated by seeds sown in heat in spring, or by cuttings of the side shoots. Araujia flowers have the power of entrapping insects, as is shown in the Plate, kindly lent with others by the editors of the *Gardeners' Chronicle*.

ARISTOLOCHIA

This is a large, polymorphic genus, chiefly tropical and most abundant in South America. The stems in many of the species are twining, and they sometimes grow rapidly to a great length. The flowers, which are exceptionally large in some species, are very remarkable in form, some, such as *A. gigas*, *A. gigantea*, *A. Goldieana*, and *A. brasiliensis*, being among the most wonderful, both as regards size and shape. Many have an objectionable odour, but when grown in a large house this is scarcely perceptible except at very close quarters. One of the most charming is *A. elegans*, the flowers of which are pleasing in form and prettily marked, and they have no odour. The best garden sorts are, in addition to those named, *A. clypeata*, *A. labiosa*, and *A. leuconeura*, the last named having large, heart-shaped, bright green leaves, with ornate reticulating yellow variegation. There are several hardy species, the best of which is *A. Sipho*, known as Dutchman's Pipe, a useful climber for covering verandahs, &c. They all like a rich soil, plenty of moisture when growing, and they love sunshine. Propagated from cuttings.

ASPARAGUS

A great many species of this widely distributed genus are twiners, their wiry stems sometimes growing to a length of 50 feet or more. They have become popular in gardens in recent years, owing to the introduction from Africa about thirty years ago of *A. plumosus*, which has proved to be a most useful plant to decorators. Another very serviceable species is *A. medioloides*, popularly known as Boston Smilax, also a native of South Africa. These two are cultivated by market gardeners, who train the stems up strings and then cut them at the base to be used in decorations. Other good climbers, suitable for clothing pillars in warm conservatories, are *A. africanus*, *A. Duchesnei*, *A. falcatus*, *A. laricinus*, *A. racemosus*, *A.*

PLATE XVI. FLOWER OF ARAUJIA SERICIFERA

Showing mode of capture of Moth.

A, pollen masses; *B*, their stalks; *C*, proboscis of moth; *D*, head of moth; *E*, portion of antenna.

retrofractus, *A. scandens*, and *A. umbellatus*. The last-named has somewhat large, star-like flowers. These plants all have fleshy roots, and they revel in rich soil, plenty of water, and a sunny position, with as much heat as they can get. Propagated from seeds or division.

BAUHINIA

A large and widely distributed genus of tropical trees or climbers, with peculiarly bilobed leaves, circinate tendrils, and usually large, showy flowers. *B. Vahlii*, the "Maloo" of India, often climbs over the tallest forest trees, and with its rope-like, twining stems sometimes strangles them. It is a useful climber for a large tropical conservatory, such as the Palm House at Kew. *B. ferruginea* is another large-leaved species which is useful in the same way. Neither of these has been known to flower in this country. *B. corymbosa* is a beautiful climber with small green leaves and flowers in corymbs on the smaller branches, the red buds and pink open flowers being very decorative. It is a native of China, as also is *B. yunnanensis*, a somewhat similar plant. These two are happy in an ordinary greenhouse.

BEAUMONTIA

Beaumontia is an Indian genus of evergreen climbers with large, opposite leaves and handsome, white flowers produced in crowded clusters on the short shoots. *B. grandiflora*, the best known, sometimes climbs to the top of high trees, and under cultivation it will, with a little management, cover a large pillar or rafter, and flower most profusely in early spring. The flowers in form and size suggest *Lilium longiflorum;* they are fragrant and they last well. In sub-tropical countries this plant is grown to cover large buildings, verandahs, and pergolas. *B. fragrans,* a recent introduction, has shorter flowers and a different calyx, otherwise it generally resembles *B. grandiflora.* The plants are all the better for an annual pruning on short-spur lines.

BERBERIDOPSIS

A monotypic genus related to the Barberry. *B. corallina,* a native of Chili, with spiny-margined leaves, and termina, drooping racemes of coral-red flowers, may be grown on a south wall in most parts of this country, and, in addition, it is worthy of a place in the cool greenhouse. It is propagated from seeds, sown in spring, by layering in autumn, or by cuttings of new wood.

BIGNONIA

A large genus of handsome American, free-growing, usually scandent shrubs, some of which have tendrils. *B. capreolata,* the Cross Vine of the Southern United States, is the hardiest, and may be grown on a south wall. It has orange-brown tubular flowers produced in summer, and slender shoots, as much as 20 feet in length. Those that are grown under glass are only suitable for large houses; they should be planted out, and trained up the back wall of a lean-to structure, or on trellis wires near the glass. Thinning the shoots so as to assist ripening of the wood is essential to a good display of flowers. *B. Chamberlaynii, B. magnifica, B. regalis, B. speciosa,* and *B. venusta* are favourites for stove cultivation. A compost of two parts fibrous loam, one of rough peat, and one of leaf mould,

PLATE XVII. BOMAREA PATACOCENSIS

Colour of flowers Carmine

and sand, is required, with good drainage. Propagation is effected by cuttings in spring, or by layering.

BOMAREA

A genus of twining Alstrœmerias, the stems in some of the species growing to a length of 20 feet or more. They resemble lilies in not developing lateral shoots, so that if a growing stem is topped it is incapable of further growth. The leaves are peculiar in being twisted on their petiole, so that they are really upside down. The flowers are produced in terminal umbels, and in some species these umbels are several feet across. They are exactly like the flowers of Alstrœmerias in form, and in colour they are invariably bright and attractive. They all grow best in a sunny, airy greenhouse, preferring a peaty soil and plenty of water in summer. Their stems will twine round a pillar with pretty effect, and when they are in flower they are most decorative. The species in cultivation are *B. Caldasiana*, *B. Carderi*, *B. multiflora*, *B. oligantha*, *B. patacocensis* (*conferta*) (see Plate XVII), and *B. Salsilla* (*oculata*). Propagated by division or from seeds.

BOUGAINVILLEA (see Plate XVIII)

The Bougainvilleas are scandent shrubs which, like some Roses, are dependent on their straggling habit of growth and stout spines for success in climbing. Like Roses, too, they may be grown, with a little management, to be self-supporting bushes. They are very popular garden plants in tropical countries, where they often form stout, woody stems and cover a large amount of space with their interlacing branches. They endure severe pruning; indeed, they are all the better for an annual spurring, particularly when they are grown up pillars or against a wall in a conservatory. The hottest house is not too hot for them, yet they can be successfully grown in an ordinary greenhouse if only they are allowed plenty of summer sunshine. Broadly speaking, the only species is *B. glabra*, but it has sported freely, the most distinct varieties being *spectabilis*, *Sanderiana*, *Cypheri*, *lateritia*, and Maud Chettleburg. The last-named has salmon-red flowers; but it is not so floriferous as the others, the best being *Sanderiana*.

BOUSSINGAULTIA

Half-hardy, tuberous-rooted plants. *B. baselloides*, the only well-known cultivated species, has alternate, entire, fleshy leaves, and long clusters of small, fragrant, whitish flowers; the rapid growing, red-tinged, twining stems produce tubercules, which are an easy means of increase. Generally grown as a climber or trailer in a warm house, to flower in autumn; sometimes also as a basket plant. A rich sandy compost and a sunny position suit it.

CÆSALPINIA

An ornamental genus of Leguminosæ, most of the species being tropical and held in little favour in this country because they are large-growing and take a long time to grow to the flowering stage. *C. japonica* (*sepiaria*), a wall-plant of spreading habit, has spiny branches, bipinnate leaves, and golden flowers with reddish anthers, produced in large, terminal racemes. *C. Gilliesii* is a beautiful

PLATE XVIII

BOUGAINVILLEA SANDERIANA

semi-hardy species not often met with. One of the finest is *C.* (*Poinciana*) *pulcherrima*, the Barbadoes Fence-Flower, a great favourite in the tropics, but not much grown by English gardeners. They are not easy to propagate, but cuttings placed under a bell-glass in heat are likely to succeed.

CALYSTEGIA

Bearbind. Hardy herbs, nearly related to Convolvulus. They are of easy cultivation, and should be trained up wires against a wall or provided with pea sticks. Propagation by means of the underground runners or by seeds. The best are *C. hederacea*, var. *flore pleno*, which has pink flowers; *C. sylvatica*, white flowers, and its rose-coloured variety.

CANTUA

Scandent South American shrubs, usually trained against walls or pillars in the greenhouse; although *C. buxifolia* (*dependens*), which has tubular, red flowers, produced in drooping clusters at the ends of the branches, may be planted out in sheltered positions in the mildest districts. *C. bicolor* has short-tubed scarlet and yellow flowers. The plants are of fairly easy culture, and are propagated by cuttings inserted in sandy soil under a hand-glass.

CASSIA

An extensive genus of yellow-flowered leguminous shrubs and herbs, few members of which are in cultivation in gardens. The best-known species, *C. corymbosa* from Tropical South America, forms a large bush, with dark green, pinnate leaves and flowers in large corymbs, and may be treated as a greenhouse climber. It is propagated by cuttings of half-ripened wood, inserted in heat during spring, and is of easy cultivation.

CELASTRUS

Staff-tree. Climbing evergreen or deciduous shrubs. The free-growing *C. scandens* is excellent for covering bowers or trellis work. It has terminal racemes of yellowish flowers, succeeded by ornamental yellow fruits. *C. articulatus* is equally valuable. They thrive in ordinary soil, and are best increased by layering the young growths in autumn. There are also greenhouse and stove species, which are propagated from cuttings of ripened wood; but these are little cultivated.

CEREUS

The climbing species of Cereus are all night flowering. They cling by means of aerial roots, and where the conditions are favourable the stems grow many feet in length. They are happiest when trained against a wall in a lean-to house, but they do well enough when fixed about a pillar or along a rafter in a warm house. Of course they must be in a position where they will get plenty of direct sunlight. They root freely in an open loamy soil, in which brick rubble has been mixed. The best known are *C. fulgidus*, *C. grandiflorus*, *C. Lemairii*, *C. Macdonaldiæ*, *C. Napoleonis*, *C. nycticalus*, and *C. triangularis*.

CEROPEGIA

A widely-distributed genus in the tropics. All the species are perennial, with a tuberous rootstock, twining stems, and

Plate XIX. CESTRUM ELEGANS

dull-coloured flowers of singular form. They are not common in gardens, their flowers appealing only to those who find interest in queer things. There is a good collection of them at Kew, where they are grown on rafters or on trellises. The showiest are *C. elegans*, *C. Monteiroæ*, *C. Sandersonii*, *C. Thwaitesii*, and *C. stapeliæformis*. They like a moist, warm house and partial shade.

CESTRUM (see Plate XIX)

Ornamental stove, greenhouse, and half-hardy shrubs, some of which are known as Habrothamnus. The favourite greenhouse species are *C. elegans* (see Plate XIX), which has downy branches and leaves, and red-purple flowers, freely produced in large terminal cymes; *C. Newellii*, much like *C. elegans*, but with scarlet flowers; and *C. aurantiacum*, with glabrous leaves and golden flowers in terminal panicles, produced in winter. Of easy culture, they should be spurred hard back after flowering. They are excellent for planting in greenhouses, to cover walls or pillars, and they repay generous treatment. They are propagated from cuttings taken in summer.

CISSUS

This genus is characterised by cymes or corymbs of small, greenish, yellow, or purplish flowers, and simple trifoliate or palmate leaves. Some authorities have sunk it in Vitis; but it is certainly better for gardeners to consider it distinct. The foliage of *C. discolor*, a native of Java, is a bright, velvety green, beautifully mottled with white, the under side deep reddish-purple, and the stems coral red. With generous treatment it is one of the best stove climbers having ornamental foliage, and may be grown either in large pots or planted out. The size and colour of the foliage is much improved by bottom heat. *C. amazonica* has attractive reddish leaves, veined with silver. *C. antarctica*, the Kangaroo Vine, introduced from New South Wales by Sir Joseph Banks in 1790, has plain green foliage, and is nearly hardy. *C. Lindenii*, a native of Columbia, and *C. Martinii*, Cochin China, which attains large dimensions, are other notable species. The king of the genus is certainly *C. pterophora* (*gongylodes*), Brazil, whose great size, handsome appearance, and singular habits are well known to visitors to the Water Lily House at Kew. The long green and red, bell-rope-like, leafy branches are trained from girder to girder, and send down whipcord-like, red roots, reaching to the water. Also, after its season of growth, each dependent branch bears at its extremity an elongated tuber; finally these drop off, and take root if circumstances are favourable. The tendrils are also very curious, exhibiting three modes of attachment—by clasping, by the discs, and by the adhesive tissue. Propagation by cuttings.

CLEMATIS

Chapter IX, p. 45, is devoted to this genus.

CLERODENDRON

Some of the tropical species of this extensive genus are climbers, *C. Thomsonæ* (*Balfouri*), which has deep red flowers with pure white calyces, abundantly produced and long lasting, being the most popular. *C. splendens* is of similar habit, with rich crimson flowers, while those of

C. speciosum, a hybrid between the two, are deep rose coloured, *C. scandens* being white flowered. These may be planted out or grown in pots, and liberally treated in a tropical temperature, with a rest in winter, when they require little or no water. Plunging the pots in bottom heat for a time when restarting growth in January or February is good for them. The climbing species are propagated by cuttings of ripened wood taken when the plants are pruned after flowering.

CLIANTHUS

An Australasian genus whose two species are distinguished as being among the most brilliantly flowered of the leguminous order. They are plants which most gardeners cultivate, but whilst one species gives no trouble the other is difficult, and many have given it up in despair. The difficult one is *C. Dampieri*, the Glory Pea, raised from seeds, has herbaceous stems, silky leaves, and bright red flowers with large purple blotches. It is propagated by grafting quite young seedlings on young plants of the Bladder Senna (*Colutea*). *C. puniceus*, the Parrot's Bill, has long, scandent shoots, green leaves, and elegant pendant racemes of scarlet flowers. It is a good pillar plant, whereas *C. Dampieri* appears to best advantage either against a south wall or as a trailer from suspended baskets. *C. magnificus* is a strong-growing variety of *puniceus* (see Plate XI). Clianthuses are generally grown under glass, but they may be seen growing out of doors as wall plants in the south-west. A good compost of loam, peat, and sand is required.

CLITORIA

Tropical evergreen leguminous climbers with axillary, pea-like flowers. There are about thirty species, wide-spread over the tropics, but few of them are in cultivation. Of these *C. Ternatea* is the best known, its flowers azure-blue with a fringed ring of white. Introduced to England as long ago as 1739, it is still a favourite in tropical collections. Clitorias are best grown from seeds, in a compost of peat, loam, and sand.

COBÆA

Fast-growing, perennial greenhouse climbers which may be grown either in pots or planted out, or outdoors as annuals. *C. scandens*, a native of Mexico, has pinnate leaves, and tubular campanulate flowers, 3 inches long, at first greenish, but changing to dark purple. The growth is so rapid that the plant is frequently employed for covering large trellises and wall areas out of doors and in large conservatories. The amount of growth a plant is capable of making in one season is prodigious. The variety *variegata* has golden variegated leaves; this is propagated by cuttings of the young shoots taken in spring. In the United States *C. scandens* is popularly known as the Cup and Saucer Vine. It is largely grown out of doors there.

COMBRETUM

Climbing or erect-growing evergreen shrubs, some of which are of considerable beauty. The climbers should be planted out in the stove to mount up pillars, and then be trained along the rafters. After flowering, the shoots require to be close pruned and thinned. Propagated by cuttings of the young side shoots taken off with a heel. *C. purpureum* has large, flat racemes of purplish-crimson flowers; those of *C. grandiflorum* are scarlet. There are said to be yellow and white flowered species.

CONVOLVULUS

Bindweed. Annual or perennial herbs and sub-shrubs, the majority being twiners. *C. arvensis*, with white or pink flowers; *C. sepium*, the common Bindweed, large white flowers; and *C. soldanella*, which has the merit of thriving in pure sand, are attractive when in flower, though perhaps chiefly notable as troublesome native weeds. Other cultivated species are *C. mauritanicus* and *C. tricolor*, the latter an annual. The greenhouse species do best in a compost of loam, leaf soil, and peat. The closely related Ipomœas are more showy plants.

DIOSCORÆA

Yam. Ornamental-leaved climbers, including both hardy and tender species, with large tuberous roots. Their white or yellow flowers are inconspicuous. In winter the roots should be stored in dry sand. The most ornamental is *D. multicolor*, of which there are varieties with prettily variegated foliage. Should be planted in a rich, loamy soil, and be liberally watered whilst growth is active. Propagated by division.

DIPLADENIA

Tropical American twiners with tuberous roots and large, trumpet-shaped, pink, red or purple flowers, freely produced throughout the summer. The favourite sorts are: *D. amabilis,* rich crimson; *D. Brearleyana,* rich crimson, very free; *D. atropurpurea,* crimson-purple with deep-yellow throat; *D. boliviensis,* white suffused with pink, and *D. splendens.* Dipladenias look best when their shoots are trained up pillars or rafters, and they may also be trained on wire trellises. They require close pruning after flowering, and to be kept warm and moderately dry during winter. Plenty of heat and moisture should be provided to induce vigorous growth in spring, when they should be replanted in fibrous peat and sand. Propagation by cuttings of the young shoots in spring.

ECCREMOCARPUS

The popular scarlet-flowered *E. scaber* will survive all but exceptionately severe winters in most places if its roots are protected. The leaves terminate in a branched tendril. It is an excellent plant for walls, trellises, and pillars, as it grows quickly, and flowers in July or August. The yellow-flowered *E. longiflorus* is also worth a place in the garden. Propagation by seeds sown in March in gentle heat; flowers being produced the same year.

ERCILLA

E. spicata, a native of Chili, is an evergreen with dark green leaves and reddish flowers abundantly produced in early summer. It clings to walls as Ivy does, and is therefore a useful outdoor plant for mild districts. Cuttings should be taken in July, and inserted in light soil under a hand-light on a warm border.

FICUS

The species that will grow on walls have the merit that, once started, they quickly cover a considerable space, and always present a fresh green appearance. *F. stipulata* (*repens*), a native of China and Japan, half-hardy, thriving outdoors in summer, is a greenhouse, Ivy-like plant, while *F. radicans* and *F. falcata,* of similar habit, should be grown in the stove. They like sandy loam, and are readily propagated by cuttings.

FUCHSIA

Some of the species attain the dimensions of small trees; thus plants of the beautiful and free-flowering *F. corallina* may be seen 20 feet in height against buildings in the west of England. Fuchsias for training on greenhouse rafters or pillars should be planted in good loamy soil, and they require to be kept dry at the roots in winter. A large exhibit of vigorous horizontally-trained fuchsias was a feature of the International Horticultural Exhibition at Chelsea. Clipper, General Greenfell, Mrs. Marshall, Mrs. Rundle, Olympia, and The Shah are the best garden varieties for growing as climbers.

GLORIOSA

The Gloriosas are tropical, tuberous-rooted plants, with lily-like flowers, in racemes on the ends of the annual stems; the petals are narrow and reflexed, and coloured red and golden yellow. The leaves have tendril-like apices. *G. superba, G. Rothschildiana* (see Plate XX), and *G. virescens* (Plantii) are the species usually cultivated. *G. Carsonii* is equally desirable. Propagation by seeds or division of the tubers. They thrive in equal parts of peat and loam. Liberal heat and moisture are essential in the season of growth, and complete rest in winter.

HARDENBERGIA

A small Australian genus with papilionaceous flowers, well adapted for training up the rafters of a greenhouse. *H. comptoniana* produces numerous racemes of purple flowers in spring. *H. monophylla* has smaller leaves and flowers, and there are red and white flowered varieties of it. Propagated by seeds, or cuttings of the firm young side shoots in spring, and cultivated in a compost of peat, loam, and sand.

HEDERA

Chapter X (Ivy), p. 56, is devoted to this genus.

HIBBERTIA

Showy climbing or bushy greenhouse shrubs, easy of cultivation, with yellow or white flowers, nearly all of them natives of Australia. The climbing species chiefly cultivated is *H. dentata*, which has thin twining stems, copper-coloured leaves, and bright yellow flowers 1½ inch across. It is a constant bloomer. *H. volubilis* has twining stems, green leaves, and large yellow flowers. A compost of peat

PLATE XX.

GLORIOSA ROTHSCHILDIANA CITRINA

Colour of flower citron-yellow and claret-purple

and loam should be used, with plenty of sand to keep it porous. Propagation by cuttings, inserted in sandy peat under a hand-glass.

HIDALGOA

A Central American genus allied to Dahlia and Coreopsis. *H. Wercklei*, the climbing Dahlia, is the only introduced species, and is a quick-growing greenhouse herbaceous climber, attaining 20 feet or more. Its flowers are bright scarlet above and yellow underneath, resembling a single Dahlia; it has elegant, much-divided leaves, and climbs by means of long, twining petioles. Propagated by cuttings.

HOLBŒLLIA

A monotypic Himalayan genus. *H. latifolia* (also known as *Stauntonia latifolia*), which may attain to 20 feet in length, and is of easy cultivation, is a good climber for a cool greenhouse. The purplish, fragrant flowers, borne in axillary racemes, appear in spring, and the foliage is thick and shining. It may be planted against a building or high wall in a warm district, but will not flower so freely as under glass. Propagation by cuttings of the half-ripened shoots in spring.

HOYA

Wax Flower. A genus comprising about fifty species, several of which are favourite stove twiners. The stems of some (notably *H. carnosa*) attach themselves to damp walls by aerial roots, as Ivy does, and are capable of thriving thus even without roots in the soil. They like peat and are easily propagated by cuttings. *H. campanulata* has elegant umbels of good-sized, amber-coloured flowers ; *H. carnosa,* pinkish-white flowers, is suitable both for the greenhouse and the stove ; *H. imperialis,* a truly noble plant, has thick leathery leaves, and reddish flowers, 3 inches across, borne in large umbels. It should be remembered that new flowers are produced on the old flower stalks as well as on the young wood.

HUMULUS

H. Lupulus, the common Hop, is a vigorous, twining perennial of great beauty when in fruit, and is sometimes to be seen employed to good effect in gardens, notably as a covering for bowers, or allowed to run wild over shrubs. *H. japonicus,* which is much like the English Hop, has a variety *lutescens* with leaves of a golden tint. Propagation by division in spring or from seeds.

HYDRANGEA

H. petiolaris (*H. scandens*) is a Japanese plant, which resembles Ivy in its mode of growth. It is quite hardy in the south, and well adapted for covering tree stumps, but requires a wall or cool conservatory in northern counties. It has white flowers, in flat-topped cymes, 8 to 10 inches in diameter. It likes a rich, loamy soil, and is increased by cuttings.

IPOMŒA (see Plate XIII)

Chiefly tropical plants resembling convolvulus. *I. purpurea* (*Convolvulus major*), and its numerous forms, *I.*

Bona-nox, I. coccinea, I. Learii, I. rubro-cærulea, and *I. versicolor* (better known as *Mina lobata,* which see) may be grown in warm places as half-hardy annuals, being raised under glass, hardened off, and planted out at the end of May. Most of the preceding, with the addition of *I. ternata* and *I. Quamoclit,* merit cultivation for summer-flowering in sandy loam in the warm greenhouse. The evergreen *I. Horsfalliæ,* which produces its beautiful rose-crimson flowers in autumn or early winter, is best propagated by layering. *I. Briggsii* is a robust, evergreen climber which in a roomy tropical house covers a large area, and flowers freely in midwinter; the flowers are rose-red in large clusters.

JASMINUM

Hardy, greenhouse, or stove-shrubs, evergreen or deciduous, mostly of climbing or trailing habit, with showy, salver-shaped, white or yellow flowers, often very fragrant. The most popular hardy species are the familiar yellow winter-flowering *J. nudiflorum,* and the white summer-flowering *J. officinale,* of which there is a variety known as *J. affine* with larger flowers. The evergreen summer-flowering *J. primulinum,* more recently introduced from Yunnan, has yellow flowers 2 inches across, and is hardy in southern gardens. *J. revolutum* (*humile*), Indian yellow Jasmine, is sufficiently hardy for wall cultivation. They like rich loam, and are easily increased by cuttings inserted under glass in July. *J. gracillimum,* from Borneo, with loose heads of fragrant white flowers, is a desirable warm house climber. *J. Sambac,* var. *flore pleno,* bearing fragrant white flowers produced at all seasons, is the best of the stove kinds; it should be planted out and trained up a pillar.

KADSURA

The only generally cultivated species is *K. japonica*, which is a not quite hardy climbing shrub, with solitary yellowish-white flowers, produced in summer, and succeeded by heads of scarlet berries; there is also a variegated form. It requires the protection of a wall, but is not particular as to soil. Propagation by cuttings of nearly ripe wood inserted in sand under a bell-glass.

KENNEDYA

An Australian genus of perennial legumes, with flowers mostly red or nearly black, which appear in spring in racemes. Those most cultivated are: *K. nigricans*, black and yellow; *K. prostrata* (*Marryattæ*), scarlet (the best of all); *K. rubicunda*, red. These are all strong growers which succeed best if planted out, but also do well when grown in pots and trained over trellises. They require liberal treatment when in active growth, and rest during winter. Propagation by cuttings or seeds in spring.

LANTANA

Naturally loose-growing shrubs, several of the Lantanas have been made to serve as greenhouse climbers, their variously coloured, Verbena-like heads of flowers being freely produced for the greater part of the year. They grow best when planted out in a sunny position in the greenhouse or conservatory. *L. salvifolia* (*delicatissima*), with pale purple flowers, is perhaps the best; it is hardy if it has the protection of a wall in the milder districts. It may also be grown as a pot shrub or as a summer bedding plant. Propagation in spring by cuttings.

PLATE XXI

LAPAGERIAS RUBRA AND ALBA

LAPAGERIA (see Plate XXI)

A greenhouse twiner with fleshy roots, and thin wiry stems which grow to an indefinite length and branch rather freely; leaves heart-shaped, dark green, leathery, the largest about 3 inches long; flowers axillary, solitary or several together, on a short pedicel, pendulous, narrow bell-shaped, about 3 inches long, sepals and petals thick and wax-like, rose-red to crimson, with numerous whitish spots; produced throughout the summer. The variety *alba* has pure white flowers. Lapageria blooms possess such substance that it is possible to keep them fresh for three weeks in a cut state, provided the water is changed with unfailing regularity. Being a native of Chili, the plant is hardy in places like South Cornwall, but it is grown most successfully in a cold greenhouse if it be planted in a well-drained bed of peat and kept uniformly moist. Care must be taken to preserve the fresh, sucker-like growths from slugs, which otherwise may eat them as fast as they come up. The Lapageria requires semi-shade. Propagated by layers.

LARDIZABALA

A small genus related to Berberis. *L. biternata*, a native of Chili, is the only cultivated species. It is a tall and fast-growing evergreen, with glossy, dark green leaves, and purple flowers in drooping racemes, notable as appearing in mid-winter. It may be planted against a wall in the milder districts in light soil, but it rarely flowers well out of doors. Propagation by cuttings of the half-ripened shoots.

LATHYRUS

A large genus, widely dispersed, and containing quite a number of desirable species which are over-shadowed by the popular Sweet Pea (*L. odoratus*). Lord Anson's Pea (*L. nervosus*), with lovely blue flowers, and *L. grandiflorus* are notable among the annual species. *L. latifolius*, rose-coloured, and its var. *albus* are perennials, attaining 5 to 7 feet, with deep-feeding roots which are patient of transplanting. *L. splendens*, "Pride of California," is a first-rate greenhouse perennial with crimson flowers, as large as those of a Sweet Pea, produced in racemes containing as many as ten. It requires a sunny position in loam and peat.

LITTONIA

A genus of Liliaceæ, of which *L. modesta*, a native of Natal, is the only cultivated species. It is a greenhouse plant with bell-shaped, orange flowers and bright, shining green leaves, and it resembles Gloriosa (see p. 95) in habit and general appearance, its cultural requirements being similar.

LONICERA

An extensive genus, confined to the Northern Hemisphere, and containing many ornamental climbers. The best hardy sorts are: *L. Periclymenum*, our common wild Honeysuckle, and *L. Caprifolium*, a naturalised species which much resembles it; *L. flava*, North America, large yellow, rather tender; *L. flexuosa*, Japan, fragrant, of pink and yellow tints; *L. japonica*, evergreen, pale yellow—vars. *aureo-reticulata* and *Halliana* are very popular; and *L. semper-*

virens, the North American Trumpet Honeysuckle, showy scarlet and yellow. These all prefer a sunny position and a rich, light soil. They should not be planted with other shrubs which will compete for soil nourishment, nor will they flower well in shade. *L. Hildebrandtiana*, a strong growing Burmese species, with large, apricot-yellow flowers; and *L. etrusca*, var. *superba*, orange-yellow, are excellent for large greenhouses. Easily propagated by cuttings or layers. Climbing Loniceras flower on the young wood.

LYCIUM

Hardy, or nearly hardy, thorny shrubs, two species of which are well known in gardens, namely, *L. chinense*, the Tea-tree or Box-thorn, which will thrive in almost any situation, and is a good seaside plant, with purplish flowers and scarlet fruits; and *L. pallidum*, from Arizona, a less vigorous grower, with peculiar greenish tubular flowers produced in May and June. Propagation in autumn or spring by cuttings.

LYGODIUM

Elegant stove and greenhouse ferns, readily distinguished by their thin, wiry, climbing fronds (stems), which are permanent and become interlaced. Those cultivated are: *L. dichotomum* (*flexuosum*), a sturdy climber; *L. japonicum*, resembling the preceding but less robust; *L. palmatum*, a cool house pillar plant; *L reticulatum;* and *L. scandens* (*volubile*), which has stems up to 15 feet. A compost of peat, loam, and sand in equal parts suits them.

MANDEVILLA

Mandevillas are tall-growing shrubs, chiefly natives of tropical America. *M. suaveolens,* the only species cultivated, is a handsome, deciduous, half-hardy plant with large, white flowers. Introduced from Buenos Aires, where it is known as Chilian Jasmine. Planted out in peat and loam in the greenhouse, and trained up the rafters, it is quite at home, and it can be grown out of doors in mild districts if some protection is afforded in winter. Propagated by cuttings of the small side-shoots.

MARCGRAVIA

A tropical American genus of epiphytal shrubs, notable for their Ivy-like habit, with two stages of growth, the juvenile stage having ovate leaves and clinging closely, while the mature stage has lanceolate leaves and does not cling. *M. umbellata* (*dubia*) is a useful wall plant for the stove. The plant known in gardens as *M. paradoxa* is *Monstera tenuis,* while that grown as *M. indica* is a Pothos. Propagated by cuttings. See also p. 69.

MAURANDIA

Mexican herbs with showy violet, purple, or rose-coloured flowers. In addition to being cultivated in greenhouses the best-known species, *M. Barclayana* and *M. scandens* and their varieties, are well adapted for covering trellises out of doors in summer, and they succeed best in moderately rich, sandy loam. Plants raised from seeds sown in gentle heat in early spring will flower the same summer if planted out in a sheltered place at the end of May.

MENISPERMUM

Moon seed. *M. canadense* is a tall and fast-growing, North American, hardy, twining, deciduous shrub of the easiest cultivation. It has large, heart-shaped leaves and long, feathery panicles of small, yellowish flowers, produced in summer, and succeeded by clusters of black berries. The only other cultivated species, *M. dauricum*, a native of Eastern Asia, is inferior. Propagated by root divisions or by cuttings in spring.

MINA

This genus of Convolvulaceæ is now included in Ipomœa. *M. lobata* (*Ipomœa versicolor*) from Mexico is frequently cultivated. It is a tall, very slender, branching, leafy climber, with twining stem and branches. The long-stalked three to five-lobed leaves are bright green above, pale beneath. The flowers, bright rosy-crimson at first, changing as they expand, first to orange, and then to pale yellow, are about 1 inch long, and borne in racemes. It may be grown in warm places as a half-hardy annual, and merits cultivation as a summer-flowering occupant of the greenhouse.

MONSTERA

Evergreen tropical Aroids. *M. deliciosa* (*Tornelia fragrans*) has stout, fleshy, scandent stems, and large, leathery, heart-shaped leaves, with numerous slit-like perforations ; is sometimes used for grouping with other plants in the outdoor sub-tropical garden. See Chapter XIII (Aroids), p. 67.

MUCUNA

Tropical Leguminosæ, with showy purple, red, or greenish-yellow flowers in axillary racemes, most of the species being tall, twining shrubs. Several are in cultivation, but they are rarely met with except in botanic gardens. The pods of *M. pruriens* and *M. prurita* are densely covered with short, intensely irritant hairs, hence their name of Cow-itch or Cow-age. *M. utilis* is known as the Velvet Bean. *M. imbricata* has great, drooping racemes of large, blackish-purple flowers, like bunches of black grapes. Mucunas require to be planted out in good loam, in a warm house, and trained near the glass. Propagation by seeds, or cuttings of half-ripened young wood.

MUEHLENBECKIA

M. complexa is a semi-hardy climber from New Zealand, with thin, wiry stems, which form a dense interlacing mass, small roundish leaves, and green, inconspicuous flowers. It requires a sunny position in well-drained or sandy soil, and can be planted to clothe a pillar or as a trailer in the rock garden. *M. adpressa*, from Australia, has larger, heart-shaped leaves and long racemes of whitish flowers. Both can be cultivated in a cool greenhouse; they require slight protection in cold winters if outdoors. Propagation by cuttings in early summer.

MUTISIA

Climbing South American Compositæ, chiefly known to gardeners because a few of the species are semi-hardy in the mildest parts of Great Britain. Nearly all have large flowers, but they are not easy of cultivation. *M. Clematis* has red flowers; *M. decurrens* is deep orange, 4–5 in. across; *M. ilicifolia* has flowers varying from white to rose, leaves holly-like; should be grown under glass. The leaves of some of the species terminate in tendrils. It is said that many gardeners have killed *M. decurrens* by planting it in hot and dry positions, whereas it requires moisture, coolness, air, sunshine, and a few slender sticks to ramble over. It grows well in South Cornwall.

ODONTADENIA

O. speciosa (*Dipladenia Harrisii*), the only cultivated species, has large racemes of trumpet-shaped yellow and orange flowers, delicately scented. The lanceolate leaves are a foot long, smooth, and dark green. Planted in a border in a tropical house is the best treatment; if grown in pots, plenty of root room and thorough drainage are necessary. Propagation by cuttings of the young shoots.

OXERA

A genus of climbing shrubs, natives of New Caledonia. *O. pulchella*, the only cultivated species, is a strong grower, with the habit of *Clerodendron Thomsonæ*, and large panicles of tubular, yellowish-white flowers, freely produced in winter. It requires a sunny position in a stove, and rich, loamy soil. Propagated by cuttings.

PASSIFLORA (see Frontispiece)

A large genus of wide distribution and great diversity of character. A few of the species have become established garden climbers, the most popular being *P. cœrulea,* which may be successfully grown either in a stove, a greenhouse, or against a sunny wall. The variety "Constance Elliott" is illustrated in the Frontispiece. It ripens its fruits freely out of doors. There are several good hybrids between this and other species, namely *P. kewensis* (*Raddiana* × *cœrulea*), *P. Munroi* (*alata* × *cœrulea*), *P. cœrulea-racemosa,* &c. The best tropical species are *P. amabilis* (*cardinalis*), *P. macrocarpa, P. quadrangularis, P. racemosa, P. Raddiana* (*Kermesina*), *P. violacea, P. vitifolia,* and *P. Watsonii.* These are all free growers, their stems are supported by tendrils, and they have showy flowers. They are satisfied with ordinary cultural conditions, and they are easily propagated by cuttings. *P. edulis, P. maliformis,* and *P. macrocarpa* have edible fruits.

PERIPLOCA

Silk Vine. *P. grœca,* the only species cultivated, is a hardy, twining, fast-growing shrub of old introduction from South Europe related to Stephanotis. It has long slender stems, which form a dense mass, and are covered with clusters of greenish-brown, hairy flowers in July and August. They have a marked unpleasant odour. Propagated by seeds or cuttings.

PETRÆA

Beautiful tropical American shrubs with opposite, coriaceous leaves, and violet-purple or bluish flowers appearing in summer. Those of *P. volubilis,* Purple Wreath, an extremely handsome twiner, are disposed in terminal, elongated, nodding racemes. *P. macrostachya* has lilac flowers in longer, pendulous racemes. Both species require rich soil and a sunny position in a stove. Propagation by cuttings in light sandy soil.

PHASEOLUS

Kidney Bean. An extensive genus, few of the species of which are of horticultural value, although *P. vulgaris* is of great importance in the vegetable garden. The Scarlet Runner Bean (*P. vulgaris*, var. *multiflorus*) is decidedly ornamental when in flower, and seedsmen offer what they call the Ornamental Runner Bean (not for culinary use), which has purplish foliage, purple and white flowers, and short, broad, purple pods. *P. Caracalla*, Climbing Snail Flower, is a tropical perennial with purple and yellowish, spirally twisted flowers, remarkably snail-like in appearance. Although universally cultivated, *P. vulgaris* is not anywhere clearly known as a wild plant.

PHILODENDRON

A large genus of Aroids, of trailing or scandent habit. Some have very large leaves, others being small and variegated. *P. Andreanum*, leaves large, shining dark green, with coppery reflections ; *P. corsianum*, leaves heart-shaped, pale green and bronze ; *P. Carderi ; P. erubescens ; P. gloriosum ;* and *P. laciniosum* (*quercifolium*) can be recommended. They require shade, with plenty of moisture and heat, and an open compost of loam or peat. Propagated by dividing the stems into three-jointed lengths, which soon take root in brisk heat ; or the tops of plants may be inserted as large cuttings.

See Chapter XIII (Aroids), p. 67.

PLUMBAGO (see Plate XXII)

Leadwort. A genus comprising hardy perennial herbs, in addition to the popular South African *P. capensis*, a scandent shrub, whose pale blue flowers are borne well-nigh continuously, and which is admirable for planting out either in the greenhouse or stove, as well as for summer bedding. There is a white-flowered variety. The flowers are produced on young wood, so that cutting hard back after flowering, and allowing the plants to rest in winter by keeping them on the dry side, are advisable. Propagation by cuttings of nearly ripe wood. The soil should be good fibrous loam, sand, and a little peat.

POLYGONUM

Differing vastly from most of its many fellows, *P. baldschuanicum* (see Plate XXIII) is a free-growing climber of considerable beauty, with sprays of rosy-tinted flowers produced in summer and autumn. It appears to best advantage when rambling over bushes, or draping some little-valued tree. It may be cut down by frost, but it soon grows again. Grafting on pieces of its own roots is the surest method of increase. The North American *P. cilinode* is a vigorous climber, which is covered with small, white flowers in autumn.

POTHOS

Tropical climbing Aroids, branching freely, the lower branchlets rooting, of spreading habit above. Few are in general cultivation. *P. celatocaulis*, Borneo, is useful for covering walls and the stems of tree ferns; its rich

PLATE XXIII. POLYGONUM BALDSCHUANICUM

PLATE XXII

PLUMBAGO CAPENSIS

dark-green leaves lying perfectly flat on the surface over which it climbs. Other ornamental climbing sorts are *P. nigricans* and *P. scandens.* It is doubtful whether several plants included under Pothos which have not yet flowered in cultivation really belong to that genus. Propagation by cuttings. See also Chapter XIII (Aroids), p. 67.

RHODOCHITON

R. volubile is an attractive greenhouse climber from Mexico, with cordate leaves, and pendent flowers with reddish calyces and nearly black corollas, freely produced. It succeeds in loam and peat. Propagation by seeds in early spring or by cuttings of the young shoots in summer.

RHUS

A large genus of chiefly hardy trees and shrubs, widely distributed, and celebrated for their poisonous properties. *R. Toxicodendron,* the Poison Ivy of North America and Japan, has large ternate leaves that colour well in autumn. Unfortunately the slightest contact between any portion of the plant and the bare skin of some people causes such a severe and long-continued skin eruption that its planting cannot be recommended. Formerly distributed as *Ampelopsis Hoggii.* Propagation by seeds or root cuttings. Plants in rich soil colour best in autumn. In America the planting of Poison Ivy is prohibited.

RHYNCOSPERMUM

Fragrant, white-flowered, evergreen shrubs, natives of Asia. *R.* (*Trachelospermum*) *jasminoides,* China and Japan, is an attractive, easily managed greenhouse climber, and hardier than was formerly thought. It should be planted in light or peaty soil, with the protection of a wall in a warm situation, and the stem should be covered if likely to be subjected to severe frost. *R. crocospermum* (*R. jasminoides angustifolia*) is hardier, with orange-centred flowers. Propagation by cutting of the young shoots in heat.

ROSA

The many beautiful climbing Roses, which—thanks in a measure to the popularity of the pergola—are now better represented in many gardens than formerly, are dealt with in Chapter VIII, p. 40.

RUBUS (see Plates IV and V)

A number of species, chiefly Chinese, are ornamental climbers. *R. deliciosus*, Rocky Mountain Bramble, one of the finest of the hardy sorts, is without spines, but will clothe a wall; it has white flowers resembling Dog Roses. *R. odoratus* is well adapted for planting under trees, has large clusters of purple flowers, and fragrant leaves. *R. phœnicolasius*, Japanese Wineberry, has scandent stems covered with reddish hairs, and its leaves are white underneath. *R. ulmifolius* has stems which attain 15 to 18 feet in length; there is a variety with double pink flowers. *R. moluccanus*, the Himalayan Blackberry, and *R. reflexus*, stems 30 feet or more, are two of the most ornamental of the more tender species, being serviceable as greenhouse pillar plants. Rubuses are easy to grow, but respond to liberal cultivation. Division or layering the young growing shoots are methods of propagation.

RUSCUS

R. androgynus (*Semele androgyna*), Climbing Butcher's Broom, a native of the Canary Islands, is very ornamental with its fresh green, pinnate foliage, like gracefully drooping branches. It thrives in any rich soil; but, attaining to very large dimensions, it is unsuitable for an ordinary conservatory, being seen to great advantage in such exceptional positions as against the circular staircase in the Temperate House at Kew. It does not object to shade.

SCHIZANDRA

A small genus of chiefly deciduous, climbing, hardy shrubs from the Far East, allied to Magnolia. The best known is *S. chinensis* (*Maximowiczia chinensis*), which attains to 20 feet, and has rosy-carmine flowers, produced in summer, and succeeded by clusters of scarlet berries, which persist during the greater part of the winter. It needs a sheltered place to do well, but is hardy in most localities if protected in winter. A rich sandy loam with partial shade is best, against a trellis or wall. Propagation by cuttings of the ripened shoots.

SELAGINELLA

A very large genus of plants with a superficial resemblance to ferns, but belonging to a different natural order (Lycopodiaceæ). Most of the species are tropical, about a hundred being in cultivation; but many of them are much alike. The only one of note as a climber is *S. Wildenovii*, a native of India, whose reddish stems attain as much as

20 feet in length, with frond-like branches 2 feet long, the scale-like leaves steel-blue in colour. With liberal stove cultivation it quickly forms a tangle of stems and branches. It requires good drainage and to be kept rather moist and shady. Propagation by stem cuttings.

SENECIO

Two species of this vast genus are meritorious garden climbers. *S. macroglossus*, Cape Ivy, is a handsome, yellow-flowered, glossy-leaved, soft-wooded evergreen, particularly well adapted for dwelling-room cultivation or planting in window-boxes as a trailer for summer display. *S. mikanioides*, German Ivy, is a yellow-flowered, much-branched climber with slender stems, which attain several feet in length, and it blossoms in winter. It is naturalised here and there on the south-west coast. Both species are easy to cultivate and propagate.

SMILAX

Green Briar. A very large genus of Liliaceæ, widely distributed, of which several species are valuable, some as greenhouse and others as hardy foliage plants. The roots of several constitute Sarsaparilla of commerce. For indoor cultivation *S. aspera*, *S. australis*, and *S. macrophylla* are generally selected. For outdoor planting, in good, dry soil in sheltered places, preferably wall-trained or rambling over tree-trunks, *S. aspera*, *S. Cantab*, *S. laurifolia*, and *S. rotundifolia* are a good selection. Propagation by root division.

SOLANDRA

Large-flowered tropical American shrubs, of which *S. grandiflora* is fairly well known in gardens. It is a vigorous grower, with fleshy branches and leaves and large, tubular, Datura-like, white flowers, which change to a creamy-yellow. An excellent plant for a sunny position in a large stove, it should be noted that if allowed too much root-space and continuous moisture it does not flower well. Small flowering plants can be had by inserting cuttings of the flowering shoots. *S. longiflora* has white flowers with a purplish tinge. *S. Hartwegii* has very large, orange-coloured flowers. Propagation by cuttings.

SOLANUM

An immense genus, many members of which have been introduced to cultivation, but few of them are notable as ornamental climbers. *S. jasminoides* (see Plate X) has wreaths of starry, white flowers, and is hardy on a wall or building in the south; in colder districts it requires and deserves green-house cultivation. *S. Wendlandii,* one of the very best of warm house climbers, has enormous, terminal clusters of bright blue-purple flowers; while *S. Seaforthianum,* mauve flowers, and *S. pensile,* purple and white flowers, are also elegant and free, summer-blooming stove plants. They thrive in loam, and are easily propagated by cuttings.

STAUNTONIA

A small genus of hardy evergreen shrubs allied to Berberis, natives of China and Japan. *S. hexaphylla,* which has small, white, fragrant flowers appearing in April, and sometimes succeeded by large, oval, purple fruits, may be grown on walls in the milder districts. Sandy loam and a sheltered position suit it, but it is liable to suffer severely if subjected to drought. Propagation by cuttings of the young, half-ripened shoots. (For *S. latifolia* see Holbœllia.)

STEPHANOTIS

A genus of Asclepiads comprising about fifteen species. Only one is well known in gardens, namely, the beautiful *S. floribunda,* the Clustered Wax Flower or Madagascar Chaplet, so popular by reason of its pure, white, tubular, fragrant blossoms, produced in great profusion, and dark green Camellia-like foliage, leathery in substance. It succeeds best planted in a small bed of turfy loam in the stove, and trained up a trellis or on the roof. Propagation in spring by cuttings of the previous year's growth. The Elvaston variety is preferred as being of compact habit, and extra-floriferous. The fruit bears a resemblance to a very large plum.

STREPTOSOLEN

S. Jamesonii, from Columbia, is a favourite sub-shrubby evergreen greenhouse plant resembling Browallia, with orange-coloured flowers in large terminal corymbose panicles, freely produced in spring. It thrives in good sandy loam. Propagation by cuttings.

STROPHANTHUS

A genus of tropical African and Asian shrubs or small trees, with quaint variously-coloured flowers, often remarkable by reason of long, tail-like expansions of the corolla lobes. *S. Bullenianus*, whose flowers combine pink, yellow, and purple, and *S. Petersianus*, var. *grandiflorus*, red and yellow, are desirable stove climbers, others of the more usually cultivated species being comparatively dwarf. They require loam and peat. Propagation by cuttings in heat.

TACSONIA

Tropical American climbers with conspicuous pendulous flowers resembling those of Passiflora, the two genera being also alike in their cultural requirements. The following are suitable for planting in a well-drained and sunny greenhouse border: *T. insignis*, large crimson flowers; *T. manicata* (*ignea*), scarlet flowers, strong-growing; *T. mollisima*, long-tubed, pink flowers; *T. Van Volxemii*, crimson flowers, very free and strong-growing; and *T. exoniensis* (*Van Volxemii* × *mollisima*). Propagation by cuttings of the young shoots in spring.

TECOMA

Trumpet Creeper. The tall-growing North American *T. radicans*, which produces very snowy orange and scarlet flowers in autumn, and clings to walls like Ivy, is hardy in most parts of the country. There are well-marked varieties in major, flava, speciosa, grandiflora, and purpurea. *T. grandiflora* (China), and its varieties, have more showy flowers and larger foliage, but are not so hardy. *T. capensis* is a greenhouse species, best treated as a pot shrub. Propagation by root cuttings, cuttings of the young shoots, or by layering. The semi-hardy Tecomas deserve to be more used as wall creepers in the milder districts. They require good, well-drained soil, plenty of sunshine to ripen the wood, abundant moisture in summer, but very little in winter. In sub-tropical countries they are popular garden-plants.

THUNBERGIA

T. alata and its varieties, with stems 4 to 5 feet long, and flowering profusely from July to October, are valuable for outdoor cultivation—treated as half-hardy annuals—in warm, sunny places; they are also popular in the greenhouse and stove. *T. grandiflora*, a strong-growing tropical species with large racemes of pale blue flowers, and its var. *alba*; *T. laurifolia*, very similar to *T. grandiflora*; and *T. affinis*, with purplish-violet flowers marked with yellow throat, form a trio for the stove. Propagated by seeds or cuttings.

TROPÆOLUM (see Plate XXIV)

Nasturtium. A South American genus, chiefly inhabiting the mountains. There are annual and perennial species, some fibrous, others tuberous-rooted. The best perennial sorts are *T. Leichtlinii*, orange flowers; *T. polyphyllum* (see Plate XXIV), yellow flowers, tuberous-rooted; *T. speciosum*, bright scarlet flowers; *T. tuberosum*, scarlet and green flowers, with slender stems, 10 to 12 feet high, not hardy in all soils. For covering arbours, &c., the tall-growing annuals, *T. Lobbianum*, *T. major*, and *T. peregrinum* (Canary Creeper), are very effective. Tropæolums flower with the greater freedom in poor soil; in better soil they make more vigorous growth, and continue in bloom much later. They are also useful for greenhouse decoration.

PLATE XXIV. TROPÆOLUM POLYPHYLLUM

The annuals are easily raised from selected seeds, sown in the open, but the double-flowered varieties can only be raised from cuttings, which are easily rooted in bottom heat. The leaves of *T. major* are eaten in salads, the green fruits are pickled, and the tubers of *T. tuberosum* are a favourite South American vegetable.

VITIS

See Chapter XI (Vines), p. 58, also Ampelopsis, p. 76.

WISTARIA (see Plates II and III)

A small genus of leguminous deciduous shrubs, natives of China, Japan, and North America, and quite the noblest of hardy introduced woody climbers. Their beauty when trained against buildings is very well known, and they are also well adapted for rambling among trees, particularly the Laburnum, which flowers at the same time. Wistarias should have good soil, and they grow fast when well established. The best species are *W. chinensis*, the first to be introduced, of which there are white- and double-flowered varieties, and the less familiar *W. multijuga*, also from China, later flowering and remarkable for its very long racemes, which sometimes exceed 3 feet in length. There are blue and white flowered varieties of this also. Propagation by layers in summer.

INDEX

THE END

5/15 Printed by BALLANTYNE, HANSON & Co.
Edinburgh & London 2½